# IRELAND: FROM EASTER UPRISING TO CIVIL WAR

# MICHAEL HODGES

B.T. Batsford Ltd  London

Typeset by Tek-Art Ltd, West Wickham, Kent
Printed in Great Britain by
R J Acford Ltd,
Chichester, Sussex
for the publishers
B.T. Batsford Ltd
4 Fitzhardinge Street
London W1H 0AH

ISBN 0 7134 5542 X

# ACKNOWLEDGMENTS

The Author and Publishers would like to thank the
following for kind permission to reproduce
illustrations: BBC Hulton Picture Library for
figures 9, 11, 15, 17, 20, 22, 23, 26, 29, 32, 35, 37,
40, 42, 48, 53, 57, 58, 59 and 60; Imperial War
Museum for figure 25; Irish Tourist Board for
figures 12 and 49; Lafayette, Dublin, for figure 51;
Mandel Archive for figures 5, 18, 27, 28 and 36;
Mander and Mitchenson Theatre Collection for
figures 41, 43 and 44; Mansell Collection for
figures 1, 2, 3, 4, 6, 13, 33, 34, 38, 39, 45, 46, 47,
54, 55 and 56; National Library of Ireland for
figures 8, 14, 24 and 52; National Museum of
Ireland for figures 16, 19, 21, 30, 31 and 50. The
maps on pages 7 and 10 were drawn by R.F. Brien.
The pictures were researched by Patricia Mandel.

The extracts from "The Rose Tree" and "Easter
1916" by W.B. Yeats (page 42) are reproduced by
kind permission of A.P. Watt on behalf of Michael
B. Yeats and Macmillan London and Basingstoke.
The extract from *Juno and the Paycock* by Sean
O'Casey (page 46) is reproduced by kind
permission of Macmillan London and
Basingstoke.

### Cover illustrations
The colour painting, by Sean Keating, shows an
I.R.A. Flying Column in the Anglo-Irish War,
1919-20 (*Crawford Municipal Art Gallery, Cork*);
the black and white print on the left is of the poet,
schoolmaster and revolutionary, Patrick Pearse
(right), with his devoted brother, Willie (*Topham
Picture Library*); the right-hand print shows an
annual Ulster procession (*BBC Hulton Picture
Library*).

### Frontispiece
I.R.A. "Irregulars" put on a show of strength in
Dublin, 1922 (*BBC Hulton Picture Library*).

# CONTENTS

# The Illustrations

# BACKCLOTH

Since 1800 England had governed Ireland directly from Westminster, with growing Irish resentment. Especially after the famine years of the 1840s many Irish people felt that only the Irish could, and should, handle Ireland's problems. Attempts to win political freedom through Parliament failed because the small presence of Irish M.P.s could never win the support of enough sympathetic English M.P.s. Even if the Irish M.P.s came near to winning enough support in the House of Commons, as they nearly did in 1886, the Conservative-controlled House of Lords was unlikely to pass a Bill which could result in one member-nation of the Empire breaking away. And two armed revolts (1848 and 1867) failed through inept planning and inadequate resources.

Then, in 1910-11 two events happened which, combined, changed the pattern of Anglo-Irish politics. First, the 1910 General Election (December) produced a "hung" Parliament. The Liberals could only stay in power by the consent of the Irish Nationalist Party. And the price of Irish cooperation was that the Liberal Prime Minister, Henry Asquith, should introduce a Home Rule Bill for Ireland. The second event was the Parliament Act (1911), which followed two years of embattled and bitter feud between the two Houses of Parliament. The Act deprived the House of Lords of its historic power to obstruct legislation. From now on a Bill sent up to the House of Lords could only be delayed for two years, after which it automatically became a law of the land.

So, when Asquith introduced the Third Irish Home Rule Bill in 1912 Ireland's age-long dream of a degree of independence was only two years away. The certainty that the Bill would become law in 1914 at once rallied the opposition. The most hostile and strident quarter was in the ancient province of Ulster, where, 300 years before, large groups of Scots and Northern English had planted themselves after driving out the native Irish. These Protestants were concentrated in the six north-eastern counties of Ulster and outnumbered the Catholic Irish by about three to two. Living with hostile, dispossessed Irish neighbours, whose religion and culture were so alien, the Ulster Protestants rejected totally the idea of Home Rule. In September

**1** Ulster citizens sign the Anti-Home Rule Pledge in Belfast's City Hall, 1912.

**2** Gun-running arms the Ulster Volunteers, a para-military "army" raised to keep Ulster out of Irish Home Rule. Arms came from Germany paid for by English Unionist sympathizers.

1912 half a million signed, some in their own blood, a solemn pledge "never to recognise a Dublin Parliament". In 1913 100,000 Ulstermen joined the para-military Ulster Volunteers who trained daily for war.

Ulster's resistance to Home Rule was supported by the Conservative Party, which upheld the Imperial status quo, and by the army establishment, which shared much the same attitudes. In March 1914 the Curragh Incident (misleadingly sometimes called "Mutiny") showed that the army could not be coerced into suppressing the loyal Protestants of Ulster, whose one wish was to stay governed by their mother Parliament in London. With military intervention apparently imminent the officers of the British garrison at the Curragh outside Dublin received a directive from the War Office that "In view of the possibility of active operations in Ulster . . . officers whose homes are in Ulster may apply for permission to be absent from duty during the period of operations." The option was not open to other officers. One hundred and fifteen officers (over 60 per cent of one division) resigned. They withdrew their resignations only when the Secretary of State for War, without Cabinet authority, gave a written assurance that the Irish Command would not be used to enforce Home Rule on Ulster.

Within the army the incident received a mixed reaction. The Director of Military Operations, Sir Henry Wilson, wrote: "These officers have won a great victory for the army . . . and will probably cause the fall of the Government . . ." while Major (later Field Marshal) A.P. Wavell was highly critical: "The army has come out badly. . . . It is a political victory. How can you call it otherwise when the army refuses to enforce the Home Rule Bill?"

The consequences of this little-known and potentially lethal situation were averted by the outbreak of the Great War, but, uncertainty of the army's loyalty, and the political interests

**3** At a Unionist rally at Blenheim Palace, 1912, Andrew Bonar Law, leader of the Conservatives, shocked many people by appearing to throw his Party behind Ulster's lawless resistance to Home Rule. But Law was pointing out that the Liberals only supported Home Rule as they needed the Irish Nationalists to stay in power. Hence Law's description of the Liberal/Irish Nationalist pact as a "corrupt Parliamentary bargain". Only about 20 Liberal candidates mentioned Ireland during the election hustings.

of famous and revered soldiers like Lord Roberts, gravely limited the options and pressure Asquith could confidently use to bring Ulster into line with the decisions of Parliament, and he was forced to make special, but unspecified, arrangments for Ulster.

Southern Ireland was outraged at Ulster's lawless opposition and by Asquith's easy capitulation. John Redmond, leader of the Irish Nationalist Party, declared, "Irish Nationalists can never agree to the mutilation of the Irish Nation." The scholar, Eoin MacNeill (pages 13-17) promptly raised the Irish Volunteers, who drew thousands to their ranks. Civil War was only averted by the outbreak of the Great War.

During this crisis the Irish Republic Brotherhood (I.R.B.) re-emerged. Formed in 1857 the I.R.B. was dedicated to overthrowing the English occupation by armed revolt. Members were called Fenians. The I.R.B. had powerful roots with the Irish

4 The Irish Volunteers were Southern Ireland's response to Ulster's war preparations.

in America. For a generation the I.R.B. had been quiet. The leaders met less to discuss action than to drink to the health of Ireland and death to England. Otherwise they brooded and waited. From the start, the large and popular Irish Volunteers movement was secretly infiltrated, and soon controlled, by I.R.B. officers. Among the most fanatical was the poet and political activist Patrick Pearse (pages 21-5). Stealthily, Pearse prepared the Volunteers for an uprising against England. MacNeill knew nothing about the I.R.B. presence in the Volunteers.

On the outbreak of the Great War Redmond urged the Volunteers to go "wherever the firing-line extends". Some Irish were offended by Redmond's readiness to align Ireland so closely to England's own problems. They argued that Ireland's freedom should not be bought with Irish lives at England's convenience. The Volunteers divided over Redmond's call-to-arms: 170,000 did indeed follow Redmond and were soon fighting in France alongside English soldiers; the remaining 10,000 broke away under MacNeill. They included the more militant Nationalists.

An old Fenian saying is "England's difficulties are Ireland's opportunities". In 1916 German victory did seem possible. Moreover, the Irish-American lobby was arranging for Germany to arm the Volunteers. With England in deep trouble in France the timing for revolt seemed perfect. The I.R.B. was convinced, anyway, that England's promise of Home Rule was a device for keeping Ireland quiet until the war was over. More distrust was felt when the chief subverter of Home Rule, Edward Carson (pages 57-60), joined Asquith's coalition government (1915). Above all, the I.R.B. felt that Home Rule – described as "a glorified County Council" by M.P. Harold Nicolson – fell far short of Irish independence. Only a "blood-sacrifice" could stir the national consciousness.

The Uprising was arranged for Easter Sunday, 23 April. Plans went wrong from the start. When the German ship carrying the arms was captured by the British navy off the

Irish coast MacNeill ordered the Volunteers to stay at home on Easter Sunday. The I.R.B. ordered the Volunteers to come out on Easter Monday instead. So, when Pearse declared the Irish Republic from the steps of the G.P.O. in Dublin the contradictory orders resulted in only 1600 Volunteers coming out – most of them in Dublin. But the surprise was complete, because only days before British Security in Dublin reported that the Irish were "sound and loyal". Irish people, too, were stunned and shocked. Most supported England's war effort and looked forward to Home Rule, which England promised after the war was over.

**5** This declaration of the Irish Republic was read out by Pearse from the G.P.O. entrance. Most Irish people were taken by surprise.

## POBLACHT NA H EIREANN.
## THE PROVISIONAL GOVERNMENT
### OF THE
# IRISH REPUBLIC
## TO THE PEOPLE OF IRELAND.

IRISHMEN AND IRISHWOMEN  In the name of God and of the dead generations from which she receives her old tradition of nationhood, Ireland, through us, summons her children to her flag and strikes for her freedom.

Having organised and trained her manhood through her secret revolutionary organisation, the Irish Republican Brotherhood, and through her open military organisations, the Irish Volunteers and the Irish Citizen Army, having patiently perfected her discipline, having resolutely waited for the right moment to reveal itself, she now seizes that moment, and, supported by her exiled children in America and by gallant allies in Europe, but relying in the first on her own strength, she strikes in full confidence of victory.

We declare the right of the people of Ireland to the ownership of Ireland, and to the unfettered control of Irish destinies, to be sovereign and indefeasible. The long usurpation of that right by a foreign people and government has not extinguished the right, nor can it ever be extinguished except by the destruction of the Irish people. In every generation the Irish people have asserted their right to national freedom and sovereignty; six times during the past three hundred years they have asserted it in arms. Standing on that fundamental right and again asserting it in arms in the face of the world, we hereby proclaim the Irish Republic as a Sovereign Independent State, and we pledge our lives and the lives of our comrades-in-arms to the cause of its freedom, of its welfare, and of its exaltation among the nations.

The Irish Republic is entitled to, and hereby claims, the allegiance of every Irishman and Irishwoman.  The Republic guarantees religious and civil liberty, equal rights and equal opportunities to all its citizens, and declares its resolve to pursue the happiness and prosperity of the whole nation and of all its parts, cherishing all the children of the nation equally, and oblivious of the differences carefully fostered by an alien government, which have divided a minority from the majority in the past.

Until our arms have brought the opportune moment for the establishment of a permanent National Government, representative of the whole people of Ireland and elected by the suffrages of all her men and women, the Provisional Government, hereby constituted, will administer the civil and military affairs of the Republic in trust for the people.

We place the cause of the Irish Republic under the protection of the Most High God, Whose blessing we invoke upon our arms, and we pray that no one who serves that cause will dishonour it by cowardice, inhumanity, or rapine.  In this supreme hour the Irish nation must, by its valour and discipline and by the readiness of its children to sacrifice themselves for the common good, prove itself worthy of the august destiny to which it is called.

Signed on behalf of the Provisional Government.
THOMAS J. CLARKE.
SEAN Mac DIARMADA.     THOMAS MacDONAGH.
P. H. PEARSE.                 EAMONN CEANNT,
JAMES CONNOLLY.          JOSEPH PLUNKETT.

**6** British troops street-fighting in Dublin during the ▶ Uprising.

For a week the Volunteers fought professional English soldiers with courage and tenacity. Outgunned and outnumbered by over 20 to one Pearse surrendered. Civilians suffered over three-quarters of the 3000 casualties. Of the military losses the Volunteers inflicted twice as many as did the English. As Dubliners looked at their devastated city they felt a deep resentment at the folly of the Volunteers. When the Volunteers were led off to captivity the streets were lined by sullen and angry citizens who jeered and taunted their fellow Irish. The prisoners would have been assaulted if the English soldiers had not been present. The Irish bishops denounced the Uprising: "a senseless, meaningless debauch of blood . . . treachery to our native land". Pearse realized the revolutionaries must endure hatred from Irish people for a time; attitudes, he believed, would change once the Irish came to understand the reasons.

After the Uprising General Maxwell was sent to govern Ireland. To him, the issue was clear: subjects of the Crown had rebelled during a national crisis and when thousands of their fellow Irishmen were doing their duty in France. Gradually it dawned on Dubliners that sinister events were taking place. On 2 May a priest and relatives of Pearse, Tom Clarke and Thomas MacDonagh were summoned by the military authorities. Next morning a terse message announced the execution of these three Volunteers.

Twelve other executions followed in the next ten days. What really horrified the Irish were the secret trials, the randomness of the executions and the clear innocence of several of the executed. For instance, Willie Pearse, a

**7** Dublin centre where the fighting mostly took ▶ place, Easter 1916. The Irish insurgents' H.Q. was the G.P.O. De Valera's H.Q. was Boland's Mill, which commanded the main approach of English reinforcements.

pacifist, was shot just because he was Patrick's brother. Most notorious was the case of Francis Sheehy-Skeffington, a much-loved Dubliner. A pacifist and a Nationalist, Francis violently opposed the Uprising, though sympathetic to the aims of the Volunteer movement. Francis patrolled Dublin to aid the wounded on both sides and to restrain his fellow citizens from looting. Francis was arrested and shot in cold blood because he had witnessed a British captain assassinate an unarmed youth. Most of the captured leaders expected to die. Tom Clarke thought of taking his own life but preferred to

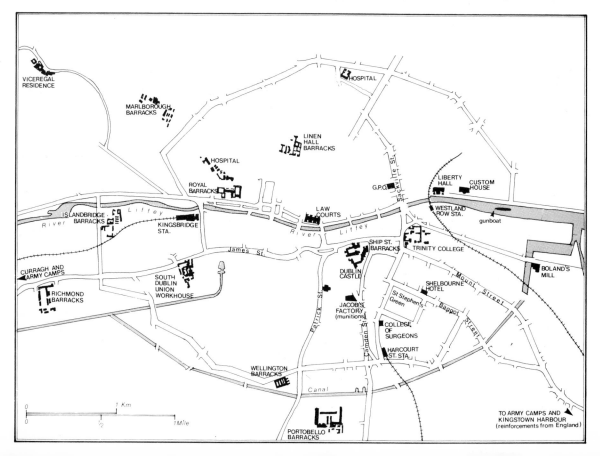

be captured, so that the guilt for his death should fall on the English.

After the fifteenth execution a Dublin woman wrote, "It was like watching a stream of blood coming from under a closed door." The reactionary Bishop of Limerick wrote to Maxwell: "Personally, I regard your action with horror and I believe it has outraged the conscience of the country." In the House of Commons the deputy-leader of the Irish Nationalists, John Dillon, facing hostile M.P.s, warned in a brave speech, "You are letting loose a river of blood."

On 12 May Asquith visited Dublin. There had been two executions that morning – and Ireland was seething with outrage. Asquith stopped further shootings. The next on the list was a young professor of Mathematics, Eamon de Valera (pages 38-40). Asquith gave the Irish brief to Lloyd George (pages 30-3). Lloyd George offered Home Rule to Southern Ireland, but not to Ulster, to take immediate effect. Redmond accepted the terms on the understanding that Ulster's exclusion was temporary. Ulster refused anything less than permanent exclusion. The talks broke down. That Home Rule seemed to be negotiated on Ulster's terms was the ruin of the one-time great Irish Nationalist Party. The pressure on Redmond to succeed suddenly became urgent. When he failed his future and that of his party were doomed. A new political party was emerging which gathered the support of moderate and extreme Nationalists alike. Sinn Féin had been founded in 1905 by Arthur Griffith (pages 17-21), with the aim of establishing, by peaceful methods, an independent Ireland under a dual monarchy. Ireland was to have its own Parliament and the people of Ireland would obey only the laws made by this Parliament. Initially Griffith's idea met with little support, but by 1917 Sinn Féin seemed increasingly relevant to Ireland's mood. Moreover, it was not tainted by association with the Home Rule negotiations.

When Redmond died a year later (May 1918) Sinn Féin had already won easily its first seat in a by-election in Roscommon (February 1917). As a gesture of good will the British had released (in June 1917) the Volunteers who had been interned after Easter 1916. They had received an enthusiastic welcome in Dublin. Among the Volunteers were de Valera and Michael Collins (pages 33-40). Both joined Sinn Féin. By the end of 1917 de Valera had succeeded Arthur Griffith as President of Sinn Féin. Many Irish now recognized Sinn Féin as the political heir to the Uprising's insurgents.

By now Irish public opinion was hostile to co-operating with England's war effort. While more and more Irish people were attracted to the now republican Sinn Féin English attitudes still clung to the Home Rule idea. So, when in April 1918 the half-expected and long-dreaded Irish Conscription Act was passed Ireland opposed it to a man. The bishops declared the Act "an oppressive and inhuman law which the Irish people have a right to resist by every means." John Dillon, who succeeded Redmond warned Lloyd George: "All Ireland will rise against you", and led the Irish M.P.s in protest back to Dublin. The Armistice (November 1918) prevented the enforcement of conscription and averted civil disobedience.

At the General Election in December 1918, Sinn Féin virtually liquidated the Irish Nationalists. The result was a clear renunciation of the Home Rule principle. Forty-seven Sinn Féin candidates, including de Valera, heard the result in prison (they had been arrested during the Conscription Crisis).

Sinn Féin now proceeded to keep their Manifesto promises. The M.P.s (called T.D.s, "Teachtei Déla") withdrew from Westminster and sat in the National Parliament ("Dáil") in Dublin. The British institutions were ignored or subverted. But a Sinn Féin delegation failed to get America's support for Ireland's autonomy at the Peace Conference. This was very disappointing, for Woodrow Wilson had declared in his presidential address that, "every people had the right to choose the sovereignty under which they live."

While the Dáil waited anxiously for

8 The police hunt after the shooting of the two ▶
policemen which precipitated the Anglo-Irish War.

England's reaction the Volunteers, now known as the I.R.A. (Irish Republic Army), killed two policemen in the R.I.C. (Royal Irish Constabulary), which still kept British law and order and which was, therefore, a natural target for the Republican gunmen. Collins, an executive of the I.R.A. and one of de Valera's key ministers, now launched a sustained wave of terror, which developed into the Anglo-Irish War. The Irish called the conflict the "Irish War of Independence", or simply "The Troubles". On 15 March 1919 the Lord Mayor of Cork, an ardent Nationalist, was shot down by a masked gang. Disquietingly, the gang spoke with English accents. It was the "Black and Tans", recruited in England to support the terrorized R.I.C. To the Irish, the "Tans" were sadists whose savagery reached a new peak of horror in Anglo-Irish history. The "Tans" were ex-servicemen whose sensitivity had become warped after four years in the trenches. They may have found the conditions of peace irksome, even stressful – like mercenary

**9** Black and Tans search Sinn Féin suspect, 1920.

soldiers today. The "Tans" were confronted with guerrilla operations conducted on a formidable scale by Collins. Unable to cope with hit-and-run tactics the enraged "Tans" took vicious reprisals on innocent civilians; though in a war of independence the "Tans" argued that every Irish person was the enemy.

On 21 November 1920, as part of the escalating scale of atrocities, 11 top British secret agents were shot down, some in front of their families, by Collins' "squad". A number of "executioners" had attended early Mass. That afternoon the "Tans" fired at random into a crowd of 8000 watching a Gaelic football match. Twelve died and 60 were wounded. On 11 December the centre of Cork was destroyed when a drunken detachment of "Tans" went on the rampage. They cut the hoses of the firemen who struggled to reach the fires.

After nearly three years of brutal war the King persuaded Lloyd George to conciliate the Irish. The King's intervention is judged by the historian A.J.P. Taylor as "perhaps the

## POLICE NOTICE.

# £1000 REWARD

### WANTED FOR MURDER IN IRELAND.

# DANIEL BREEN

(calls himself Commandant of the Third Tipperary Brigade).

Age 27, 5 feet 7 inches in height, bronzed complexion, dark hair (long in front), grey eyes, short cocked nose, stout build, weight about 12 stone, clean shaven; sulky bulldog appearance; looks rather like a blacksmith coming from work; wears cap pulled well down over face.

The above reward will be paid by the Irish Authorities, to any person not in the Public Service who may give information resulting in his arrest.

Information to be given at any Police Station.

greatest service performed by a British monarch in modern times" (*English History 1914-45*). A truce was declared on 11 July 1921.

On 6 December of that year the Anglo-Irish Treaty was signed after hard, tough bargaining. The Irish won a settlement which was far more than the brilliant politician Parnell (page 68) of the last generation and his successor, Redmond, ever sought; but it was less than the Irish had recently fought for. Ireland had to acknowledge British sovereignty. Ulster was included in the new Irish state, with the choice of opting out after one month, which the six Protestant counties proceeded to do. This odd arrangement

**10** Two Irelands.

— · — · — Historic Ulster boundary

———— Partition boundary

showed that the British Government accepted the principle of a united Ireland.

People felt that the six Ulster Unionist counties under their Belfast Parliament could not survive politically and, in time, would return to Ireland. The Boundary Commission clause, which at a future date would arbitrate on North-South boundary adjustments, reassured the South that Ulster's secession was not permanent; Ulster, of course, thought otherwise. Northern Ireland was partitioned and remains part of the United Kingdom to this day.    The T.D.s endorsed the Treaty by just seven votes. De Valera denounced the talks and refused to take the oath of allegiance. Griffith replaced him as President of the Dáil. Michael Collins became leader of an uneasy Sinn Féin Government.

Disaffection with the Treaty spread to the I.R.A. Taking the law, and arms, into their own hands, groups of the I.R.A., including de Valera, declared war against the Irish Free State. After nearly a year of vicious civil war de Valera ordered the Anti-Treaty I.R.A. groups to surrender. By that time Griffith had died and Collins had been killed. In the last few months of the war William Cosgrave took over the government and adopted a ruthless policy against the I.R.A. dissidents. Political assassinations and reprisals, internment and execution without charge or trial were commonplace. Irish casualties were higher than in the recent wars with England. But the real casualty was Ulster. During "The Troubles" in the South Ulster had maintained her entrenched position. The terrible fratricidal war in the South bore out all the fears Ulster had ever felt for unity with the South. Kevin O'Higgins, Minister for Home Affairs, in the Sinn Féin Government lamented:

We had an opportunity of building up a worthy State that would attract and, in time, absorb [Ulster] . . . and now we wonder why the Orangemen are not hopping across the Border to come within our field of jurisdiction.

# VISIONARIES

Two stumbling-blocks to Irish independence were the virtual extinction of the Irish language and the dependence of the Irish Nationalist Party on the English political parties, usually the Liberals. From the beginning of the century three Irishmen began to challenge this position.

Eoin MacNeill founded the Gaelic League, which successfully revived Irish literature and history. MacNeill might have been remembered just as a highly respected scholar who returned the Irish language to the Irish people. As it was, he became more and more involved with the tense politics of the day and was drawn, inevitably, into the unbending policies of the I.R.B.

Arthur Griffith's vision was an independent Ireland with a dual monarchy – an Irish and an English Crown to reconcile all shades of British and Irish opinion. But, now that Home Rule was within their grasp the Irish were unlikely to desert their leader, John Redmond, for Griffith's rather abstract model. And the I.R.B. denounced any Irish movement which tolerated even a tenuous link with England. For ten years Griffiths and Sinn Féin, the political movement he founded, were isolated from mainstream politics.

Patrick Pearse was a poet and political activist. He and a small band of literate, dedicated revolutionaries became very impatient with the moderate polices of MacNeill and Griffith. "We never meant to be nothing more than Gaelic Leaguers," Pearse wrote in 1913. "The League was a prophet, but not the Messiah." Pearse himself adopted the Messianic role in the sense that he sacrificed his life to shake Ireland out of her political apathy. From 1912 Pearse was committed to an uprising, even though it meant running against the tide of Irish public opinion.

## Eoin MacNeill (1867-1945)

Eoin MacNeill was born into a Catholic family in County Antrim, where the population was overwhelmingly Protestant. From early on his interests lay in Irish history and literature. He believed that Ireland could never reach a genuine state of nationhood until she was free of English influences. MacNeill's close collaborator, Douglas Hyde, son of a Church of Ireland rector, had faced up to this ancient Irish problem in a lecture called "The Necessity for De-Anglicising Ireland" (1892).

It has always been very curious to me how Irish sentiment continues to apparently hate the English, and at the same time continues to imitate them.

The Gaelic League, founded in 1893 by MacNeill and Hyde, aimed to regenerate the glory of Irish culture and, by so doing, to re-assert the Irish feeling of nationality. Every summer MacNeill took his family and groups of friends to the Aran Islands off Galway.

There they learnt Irish in an atmosphere and among people that hadn't changed since the time of Christ. MacNeill would return to Dublin with Gaelic-speaking nannies so that his children could grow up speaking Irish in an English-speaking Dublin. The Gaelic League also revived traditional Irish games such as hurling, Irish customs and manners, surnames and place-names. Before long, around 600 branches had sprung up throughout Ireland. One major practical achievement of MacNeill and his Gaelic League co-founders was the introduction of the teaching of Irish in primary schools.

In 1913 MacNeill's scholarship was recognized: he was appointed Professor of Early Irish History at the National University. His reputation went well beyond academic circles. His grass roots' work for the League, involving many miles and long hours of travel, brought him into touch with ordinary people.

◀ **11**  Eoin MacNeill (right) and Douglas Hyde founded the Gaelic League.

**12**  The Aran Islands off Co. Galway. Here MacNeill stayed during the summer among Gaelic-speaking Irish.

They too, admired and respected him. MacNeill's prospects certainly seemed settled and predictable. However, some people who had become fascinated by MacNeill and drawn into the League's activities argued that the Gaelic League was too detached from politics. One of these people, William Rooney, co-founder of Sinn Féin with Arthur Griffith, told MacNeill it was a mistake to avoid politics,

. . . in any organisation which has charged itself with the promotion of Irish nationality. . . . You couldn't promote language without agitation but agitation means politics and the movement [Gaelic League] has got to face it, if it is not to come to a stand still.

In fact, MacNeill's politics were thought to be moderate. He had supported Redmond over the Home Rule Bill provisions, though MacNeill ended his speech welcoming the Bill with a warning:

**13** Teaching Irish revived Irish nationalism. Here, nuns are taught Irish by a member of the Gaelic League.

There is no law so very bad that it would not be better for the Irish people to accept if they themselves were in charge of it. If the English people have sense they will not keep back from Ireland as much as one inch of her rights. We are not asking for charity but demanding our rights.

On 1 November 1913 MacNeill published an article in the Gaelic League journal, *An Claidheamh Soluis* ("Sword of Light"), which was to change his position in Irish affairs. MacNeill's article called "The North Began" was a response to the newly raised Ulster Volunteers:

Ulster has shown the way and made it clear that the British army cannot now be used to prevent the enrolment, drilling and reviewing of Volunteers in Ireland.

It is evident that the only solution now possible is for the Empire to make terms with Ireland or to let Ireland go her own way. In any case it is manifest that all people Unionist as well as Nationalist are determined to have their own way in Ireland.

MacNeill's challenging words, coming from a well-known and moderate man, were a complete surprise. "Many people," wrote the historian Leyland Lyons in *Ireland Since the Famine*, "were prepared to pay attention to what he said, but when what he said turned out so different from what he might have been expected to say, the impact was all the greater." Nowhere was the impact greater than with that extreme Republican movement, the I.R.B. The I.R.B. at once grasped the implication of the "physical force" idea, which was always a means to the I.R.B. ends. MacNeill was urged by I.R.B. officials to take his initiative further. On 25 November MacNeill addressed an audience of 8000 in the Rotunda Rink, Dublin. He told the meeting: "They have rights who dare maintain them."

He appealed for "a body of Irish Volunteers", whose duties would be "defensive and protective" and whose object would be "to ensure the rights and liberties common to all the people of Ireland". That night 4000 joined the Irish Volunteers. Ten months later MacNeill was president of 180,000 Volunteers.

Behind the benign and unsuspecting MacNeill the I.R.B. manipulated the Volunteers for the planned Easter Rising. MacNeill didn't know that the I.R.B. had penetrated the Volunteers at the highest policy level. However, rumours of a Rising became so widespread that four months before Easter 1916 MacNeill publicly declared his own policy on any proposed revolution:

Success must be success in the operation itself,

**14** MacNeill inspired the formation of the Irish Volunteers. The different clothes show that the Volunteers attracted men from all walks of life.

not merely some future moral or political advantage which may be hoped for as the result of non-success.

On the eve of the Easter Uprising, when the German ship carrying arms was lost off the Irish coast, Pearse refused to withdraw the I.R.B. plans. But MacNeill published a notice in the *Sunday Independent* which ordered the Volunteers not to take up arms:

Owing to the very critical position, all orders given to Irish Volunteers for Easter Sunday are hereby rescinded, and no parades, marches, or other movements of Irish Volunteers will take place.

MacNeill's instruction caused a lot of confusion but most Volunteers obeyed him. Some Volunteers never forgave MacNeill for opposing the Uprising, but, in spite of the angry exchanges before the Uprising between the I.R.B. and MacNeill, neither blamed the other afterwards. The conspirators appreciated that MacNeill acted consistently and courageously. At MacNeill's court-martial after the round-up of all Volunteer leaders, and in later years, he defended the honour and motives of Pearse and his I.R.B. colleagues.

MacNeill was sent to Dartmoor prison. He arrived at a time when other Volunteer prisoners were lined up for roll-call. One prisoner remembered this occasion:

We were all conscious that the prisoners had

mixed feelings about him [MacNeill], as he had stopped the Rising. To our amazement Eamon de Valera stepped out from our ranks and faced us. His voice rang out: "Irish Volunteers! Attention! Eyes left!" The command – a salute for MacNeill – was obeyed with military precision!

On his release from prison later that year MacNeill campaigned for de Valera. MacNeill joined the Sinn Féin government of 1918 and was Minister for Education in the Pro-Treaty Government. MacNeill's last political job was to represent the Free State on the Boundary Commission which met in 1924 to consider changes of the border territory. After a year's sitting, and silence, a newspaper leak (in November 1925) revealed that only very small adjustments were planned, including the transfer of a strip in East Donegal to Ulster. MacNeill resigned, but far too late to avoid suspicion that he had failed to fight hard enought for the Free State's interests.

From then on MacNeill faded from public affairs. He lost his parliamentary seat in the 1927 election and returned to the life of a scholar, where he was happiest and, probably, most effective. His last job was Chairman of the Irish Manuscript Commission.

To the end, he was haunted by the Easter Uprising. His decision may have been right – if Pearse had waited two years events might have been very different. Ulick O'Connor (born in 1924) a barrister and writer, recalls his grandfather, who knew MacNeill, saying, "Remember, when you grow up, MacNeill was a good man."

# Arthur Griffith (1871-1922)

Winston Churchill once described Arthur Griffith as, "that rare phenomenon, a silent Irishman". Some people were indeed put off by his forbidding and withdrawn presence.

He could be abrasive and critical, especially of Irish servitude to England. Home Rulers were one group who quailed beneath Griffith's harsh words. Griffith's few close friends were devoted to him. Nothing relaxed him more than singing with his friends popular or, better still, unknown Irish folksongs which he had picked up from his wanderings in the twilight around the neighbourhood of St Patrick's Cathedral, Dublin, where his hero, Jonathan Swift, had once been Dean.

Arthur Griffith came from a line of Dublin tradesmen. He himself was a printer. He dabbled early in Irish politics and emigrated to South Africa. He returned to Ireland in 1899 to edit a new magazine, *United Ireland*, which came to have a powerful effect on Irish people. The historian Leyland Lyons, in *Ireland Since the Famine*, wrote of him:

**15** Arthur Griffith's political vision made more sense after the Uprising.

Griffith was an inspired journalist, who combined style and temper no one else could match. He recalled the savagery of Swift to which were added his own intensity and his own intimate knowledge of the political and economic environment about him.

From the start Griffith was on the police files for campaigning against the recruitment of Irishmen into the British army. He mocked the visit in 1900 of the aged Queen Victoria, "in her dotage . . . to seek recruits for her battered army" (at the hands of the Boers). Griffith attracted distinguished and varied contributors (one was the poet W.B. Yeats). The directness and fluency of his editorship reached a very wide readership. The conversion to the Irish cause of independence of famous Anglo-Irish like Roger Casement, the poet James Stephens, Countess Markievicz, and the actress Maud Gonne was influenced by what they read in *United Ireland*.

Griffith's vision was to reconcile all the minority sectors of Irish society – Ulster Protestants, Southern Unionists and those Catholic Irish who were conditioned to the union with England. Griffith envisaged an independent Ireland under a dual monarchy. The British sovereign would break down the anxieties of the Unionists; the King of Ireland would provide a unifying force and distinctiveness for all Irish ethnic and religious groups. Griffith knew the Irish well. If he had urged a complete severance with Britain he would have lost some Gaelic Irish as well as the Unionists. "I am a separatist" he said, "but the Irish people are not separatists. I think they can be united under this policy." Within this Imperial framework Griffith proposed that all Irish M.P.s should withdraw from the Westminster Parliament. Ireland, therefore, would become responsible for all aspects of self-government. Griffith called his political movement Sinn Féin (1905), which means 'Ourselves'. The name sums up Griffith's philosophy of a self-reliant Ireland.

The inspiration for Griffith's political model came from the experiences of the Austro-Hungarian Empire. In 1848 Hungary revolted under Franz Déak and became an autonomous and constitutional monarchy within the Hapsburg Empire, whose Emperor the Hungarians acknowledged. The historic parallel was not exact: what mattered was that the idea caught the imagination of many Irish people. Yet, in spite of its ingenuity, the notion failed to make any practical progress until after Easter 1916. The idea went too far for most Irish, who were satisfied with Redmond's Home Rule provisions, while for the Republicans it did not go far enough. For some years Griffith was in the political wilderness.

Griffith had been a member of the I.R.B. until 1906, but he was against violence and strongly opposed the Easter Uprising until he found himself so inspired by the insurgents' ideals that he offered to join them at the barricades. He was urged not to by the Republicans as his propaganda work was so vital for the future. As it happened, practically everybody thought, mistakenly, that Sinn Féin was behind the Uprising. Griffith's innocence did not prevent his arrest, but this did his reputation no harm, especially in the eyes of the I.R.B. to whom a spell in prison

was fast becoming an essential sign of patriotic commitment. Griffith was released at the end of 1916. He at once returned with all his old vigour to attacking the issues of the day: the threat of conscription and the partition of Ireland.

Once Redmond's Irish Nationalists failed to achieve an all-Ireland Home Rule under Lloyd George's 1916 initiative Sinn Féin seemed increasingly relevant to Ireland's mood. By October 1917 Sinn Féin membership had grown massively to a quarter of a million, from a mere 11,000 the previous April. In July 1917 all the prisoners of the Uprising had been released as a show of England's good will. They returned to Ireland to a hero's welcome, to Dublin streets lined with Republican flags and with a commitment to independence.

Griffith realized that the I.R.B. and the Volunteers needed a political outlet so that the aims of Easter 1916 could be sustained. The

**16** Irish Volunteers released from internment (1917) received a heroes' welcome in Dublin. Griffith's Sinn Féin soon provided a political outlet for the Volunteers.

I.R.B., too, saw the sense in some kind of association with the popular and ever-growing Sinn Féin. At a convention (25 October 1917) 1000 delegates from Sinn Féin, the I.R.B. and the Volunteers met to agree on a common policy for Ireland. Sinn Féin and the I.R.B. each provided one important advantage which the other needed: Sinn Féin possessed the political inspiration and a growing credibility with the country; the I.R.B. had the aura of Easter 1916 and the two surviving leaders, Eamon de Valera and Michael Collins. But there was resentment between the two groups. For instance, the I.R.B. could not easily forgive those who hadn't "come out" at Easter 1916. Nor was it forgotten that Griffith had initially opposed the Uprising. But Griffith had come to terms with violence as a means to maintain the South's precarious independence. Like MacNeill, however, Griffith saw no point in violence without certain political success at the end of the day. Now that Ireland was more united behind Sinn Féin than she had been behind the Easter insurgents the right moment for "physical force" had arrived. That the convention did not deteriorate into squabbling was due to the wisdom and generosity of Griffith. He stood down as President of Sinn Féin in favour of de Valera. "A great leader," said Griffith of de Valera: "a man with a wonderful judgement such as I have never met in a young man except in Parnell".

Sinn Féin was now the official political heir to the revolutionaries of 1916. The Volunteers were reorganized with de Valera as President. So, when Sinn Féin won the vast majority of Irish seats in the December 1918 General Election Ireland had an army (soon to be known as the I.R.A.) which was already closely linked with the elected government.

Returning to Dublin in 1921 with the signed Anglo-Irish Treaty Griffith urged the Dáil to accept the terms:

We have brought back the evacuation of Ireland after 700 years by British troops and the

**17** Leaders of the first Sinn Féin Parliament, 1919. Griffith is seated fourth from left, Collins is second from left, de Valera is in the centre, and MacNeill is third from right.

formation of an Irish army. We have brought back to Ireland equality with England, equality with all nations which form the Commonwealth, and an equal voice in the direction of foreign affairs in peace and war.

This was an impressive performance and it won a narrow majority in the Dáil. But it failed to impress 57 T.D.s, including de Valera and Childers.

In their own speeches de Valera and Childers exposed the fallacy of the Treaty – the Oath of Loyalty still made Ireland dependent on England. That fact was unacceptable to enough Irish people for them to wage the ten-month civil war in which Griffith was President of the Irish Free State. To Griffith the civil war was a terrible and bitter personal blow. A few years before his political vision for Ireland seemed hopelessly irrelevant. Then, in 1917, Griffith's idea seemed the best hope. And now his great vision was being torn apart before his eyes by the Irish themselves.

More tragic still, Griffith had already worked out a scheme whereby half the seats in the Senate would be allocated to the southern Unionists who "were not adequately represented in the Dáil". The most promising politician of the up-and-coming generation, Kevin O'Higgins (Minister for Home Affairs), endorsed Griffith's policy towards the English settlers (page 49):

It comes well from us to make a generous adjustment to show that these people are regarded, not as alien enemies, not as planters, but that we regard them as part and parcel of this nation, and that we wish them to take their share of its responsibilities.

On 12 August, at the early age of 51, Griffith died of a heart attack – more likely of a broken heart.

# Patrick Pearse (1879-1916)

There has been nothing more terrible in Irish history than the failure of the last generation.

Pearse was reflecting on Ireland at the beginning of the twentieth century. He felt that the Irish Nationalist movement and its submissive approach to England would never achieve the kind of independence that true Irish people wanted. Pearse's statement suggests, too, that he was not prepared to support the traditional methods of Irish politicians which led to this "failure".

Patrick Pearse was born in Dublin, the son of an English sculptor who had been invited by Cardinal Newman to work on a new church in Dublin. Pearse qualified as a lawyer but never practised. He first showed his dissent from the English occupation of Ireland by founding his own bilingual school, St Enda, in 1908. Here the pupils learnt the Irish language and read Gaelic literature; they played the ancient Irish game hurling. All the while, Pearse was indoctrinating the next generation of patriots, and martyrs, with his extreme republican ideas. Over the doorway of St Enda the words "I care not that I live but one night and one day, if my deeds shall be remembered for ever" reminded every pupil of the legendary Ulster hero Cuchulain, who died fighting alone against overwhelming numbers of the invader.

At about this time Pearse wrote:

We must be ready to die even as Emmet [an

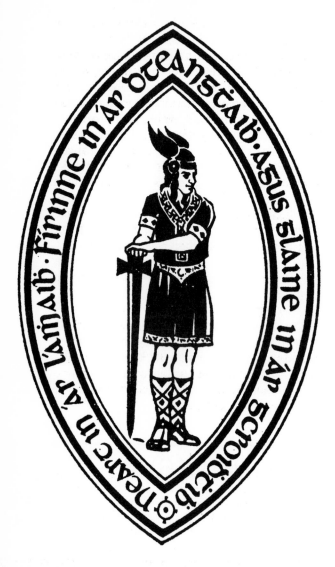

reflected in this poem, "The Mother", which he wrote from a mother's point of view:

I do not grudge them; Lord I do not grudge
My two strong sons that I have seen go out
To break themselves and die; they and a few,
In bloody protest for a glorious thing.
(From *Patrick Pearse's Plays, Stories, Poems*, Dublin 1924)

Before long Pearse's activities extended to national affairs. In his speeches Pearse struggled to nationalize Irish opinion to win political freedom on Irish terms. Though a shy, and to some an aloof, man, who possessed a slight stammer, his speeches enthralled many people. Others were very disturbed by his violent language and lust for a blood sacrifice. Pearse was one of the public speakers who addressed the huge crowd in O'Connell Street on 31 March 1912 to welcome Redmond's Home Rule Bill. The crowd warmly applauded Redmond's message. "Trust the old party – and Home Rule next year." Then came Pearse, who introduced a more menacing tone. After a conciliatory opening, Pearse ended:

But if we are tricked this time, there is a party in Ireland that will advise the Gael to have no counsel or dealings with the Gall [English] for ever again but to answer them hence forward with the strong hand and the sword's edge. Let the Gall understand that if we are cheated once more there will be red war in Ireland.

**18**  The crest of St Enda School, founded by Pearse.

eighteenth-century patriot] died on the gallows, as Christ died on Calvary, so that the people may live.

These revealing words indicate that Pearse was thinking quite early on of an armed revolt against England. To a devout Catholic like Pearse, Christ's sacrifice for mankind could inspire people to sacrifice their lives for the freedom of their country. This theme recurs in Pearse's political writings and poetry. Pearse's attitude to self-sacrifice for a noble cause is

Pearse's oratory and his magnetic presence impressed people who had no sympathy with Home Rulers. One such was Tom Clarke a tough, middle-aged Fenian with 20 years' suffering in English prisons behind him. Clarke kept a tobacconist shop in Dublin where the I.R.B. leaders used to meet to discuss plans for revolution and hear about support from Irish friends in America. By December 1913 Pearse was himself a member of the I.R.B. and attended the meetings in Clarke's shop.

In 1913 a series of grim strikes brought industrial Dublin to a standstill for six months. Marches and crowds were broken up by excessive police brutality in which some citizens lost their lives. In these circumstances Pearse came face to face with the desperate squalor of Dublin's poor, and he met the socialist trade union leader, James Connolly (pages 26-30). At first Connolly and Pearse had little understanding of each other. Their background was quite different, and their proposed solutions to Dublin's poverty were very different, too. Pearse said:

Before God, I believe that the root of the matter [poverty] lies in foreign domination. A free Ireland would not, and could not, have hunger in her fertile vales and squalor in her cities.

Connolly did not believe that a free Ireland would resolve poverty; for him the only answer was socialism. However, preparations for an uprising brought Pearse and Connolly closer together – as did their deaths.

Very soon Pearse, with his poet friends MacDonagh and Plunkett, was elected to the military council of the I.R.B. and they occupied the three most important military jobs in the Volunteers movement. As the tension in Ireland grew Pearse became increasingly obsessed with armed revolt and the need for a "blood-sacrifice". When the Ulster Volunteers were arming and training for war Pearse wrote:

I am glad the Orangemen have armed. We must get used to arms. Bloodshed is a cleansing and sanctifying thing, and the nation which regards it as the final horror has lost its manhood. There are many things more horrible than bloodshed, and slavery is one of them.

In the summer of 1915 Pearse was invited to deliver the funeral oration over the grave of an old Fenian, one O'Donaghue Rossa, who had recently died in America where the English had exiled him 40 years before. Rossa was not a particularly famous Fenian – in fact one colleague from the 1860s had said that Rossa couldn't be trusted to burn a haystack. Rossa had certainly been staunchly republican and had led bomb attacks in England, but in his old age he had modified his extremism to the point of supporting the Home Rule lobby. His funeral assumed national importance because it attracted all shades of political opinion. Redmond's Nationalists were present, for they could forgive a once violent man who had been tamed. The I.R.B. were present because Rossa was a symbolic figure and the occasion could be exploited to serve republican interests. Both Redmond's and MacNeill's Volunteers marched that day in long columns and thousands of civilians filed past the grave. So when Pearse in Volunteers' uniform spoke it looked as though he spoke for all Ireland. The speech was one of his most moving:

. . . from the graves of patriot men and women spring living nations. . . . The English think that they have pacified Ireland. They think that they have purchased half of us and intimidated the other half. . . . They think that they have provided against everything; but the fools, the fools, the fools! – they have left us our Fenian dead, and while Ireland holds those graves, Ireland unfree shall never be at peace.

**19** The G.P.O. at the height of the Easter Uprising. Pearse stands (hatless) on the left of the stretcher, where Connolly lies wounded. Note the artist has caught the "romance" of the occasion. Compare this visual impression with O'Casey's description (page 47).

In spite of MacNeill's pleas Pearse refused to stop the Easter Uprising:

It is no use trying to stop us: our plans are all made and will be carried out.

On Easter Monday 1916 Pearse stood on the steps of the G.P.O. and to a small and bewildered crowd announced that the Irish Republic had replaced English rule:

We declare the right of the people of Ireland to the ownership of Ireland. . . . The long usurpation of that right by a foreign people and government has not extinguished that right. . . . Standing on that fundamental right we proclaim the Irish Republic as a sovereign independent state.

Just before Pearse surrendered a week later he said prophetically to the Volunteers near him:

People will blame us for everything, condemn us; but for this protest the War would have ended and nothing would have been done. After a few years, they will see the meaning of what we tried to do.

At his court martial Pearse defended himself with dignity:

I assume I am speaking to Englishmen who value their own freedom, and who profess to be fighting for the freedom of Belgium. We too love freedom and desire it. If you strike us down now we shall rise again and renew the fight.

And, in a letter to his mother written hours before his execution, he said:

**20**  British troops occupy the ruins of the G.P.O.

KILMAINHAM MAY 1916

We have done right. People will say hard things of us now, but later on will praise us.

The execution of the patriots very soon created a sense of national guilt, just as Pearse had predicted – and desired. They were the first of their generation of patriots to die but they have survived the longest. Today's Provisional I.R.A. see themselves as descendants of the Irish who declared the Republic in 1916, and heirs to their objectives. The Provisional I.R.A. accept violence and the need for a "blood-sacrifice" to achieve a united Irish Republic just as Patrick Pearse did. The day after Pearse was executed George Bernard Shaw (the Irish playwright) wrote to the *Daily News*:

**21** Reprisals. Fifteen revolutionaries were executed, including the seven men who proclaimed the Irish Republic. Of these seven leaders, four were writers, including the very promising Thomas MacDonagh and the aristocratic and eccentric Joseph Plunkett. The night before Plunkett died he was married in the prison chapel to Grace Gifford.

The shot Irishmen will now take their places beside Emmet in Ireland, and beside the heroes of Poland and Serbia and Belgium in Europe, and nothing in heaven or earth can prevent it.

Already the consequences of the Uprising were beginning to take shape.

# POLITICIANS

Jim Larkin and James Connolly founded the Irish Labour Movement. Their aim was to improve the lot of the Irish worker, but this conflicted with the political objectives of the nationalist movements. Griffith deplored direct action by workers because it brought hardship to labour and deflected Ireland from the primary aim of achieving political independence.

Connolly was equally suspicious of the nationalist movements, directed in the main by the middle-classes, with their narrow political aim in which the place of labour was not explicitly stated. The last thing Connolly wanted was a revolution which might change the political masters but left the workers floundering where they were. Gradually, Connolly saw that the political Nationalists were complementary to his socialist ideals. By 1916 Connolly was echoing Larkin's response to the republican movement: "Why use one arm when we have two? Why not strike the enemy with both arms – the political and the economic?"

After the Uprising and the execution of the leaders the political momentum was carried on by de Valera and Collins. They integrated the more extreme aims and methods of the revolutionaries with Sinn Féin. Lloyd George was asked by Asquith to find a solution. By 1921 Ireland had become far more independent than was thought possible in 1916. By the end of the 1930s de Valera had thrown off the few links which under the 1921 Anglo-Irish Treaty bound Ireland to England. Twenty-six of Ireland's 32 counties were republican.

While Ireland made dramatic political progress in these few years the position of the Irish worker was as depressed as before, just what Connolly had spent and given his life to avoid.

## James Connolly (1868-1916)

Many people testified to the abysmal conditions of Dublin's working class at the beginning of the century: "Behind the splendour of the Georgian drawing-rooms, the excitement of the literary revival, Dublin had this private shame", wrote the historian Ulick O'Connor in *A Terrible Beauty is Born*. The conservative *Irish Times* compared the lot of Dublin's poor with Dante's *Inferno*. Thirty per cent of Dubliners (87,000) languished in tenement slums without heat, light, sanitation or water. A priest told a Royal Commission that over 20,000 families lived in one room per family. The tenements are described by one of Sean O'Casey's characters as "vaults that are hidin' the dead instead of homes that are shelterin' the livin'".

For some years Dublin had been drawing in thousands of rural labourers. The economic base of Dublin was almost entirely services and distribution. Very little manufacturing industry existed able to absorb this influx of labour. A debilitated wage-earner, high infant mortality and the highest death rate in any European city, even exceeding Calcutta which had to contend with the plague and cholera, were all the consequences of high unemployment, "sweated" labour (long hours and low wages – £1 per week in 1910), malnutrition, and cramped and poor dwellings. Another consequence was the emergence of two great labour leaders, who with reforming zeal struggled to secure a better deal for the impoverished and dulled labourer. One was Jim Larkin, who united the Dublin proletariat (dockers, carriers and labourers) by forming the Irish Transport and General Workers Union (ITGWU). Larkin "could lift the people from their knees with a brilliant phrase, and had a voice that could carry across the prairies". The second great labour leader, James Connolly, was even more formidable.

James Connolly was born and brought up in grinding poverty in Edinburgh, where his family had emigrated from Ireland. He had no

**23** James Larkin inspired Connolly's socialism. ▲

**22** James Connolly was a leading figure in the Irish Labour movement. He joined the Uprising with misgivings because he felt a political revolt would not help the workers. ▼

formal education and spent his early years working in dead-end jobs. He went to America between 1903 and 1911, where he observed the system of American trade unionism at first hand. Though he was repelled by the in-fighting he saw the value of organized labour and economic pressure as a means to redress the grip of capitalism on labour. The direct action of workers, which included escalating strikes, was called "Syndicalism". He read deeply into socialism, which he was the first Irishman to try to apply to Ireland. His book *Labour in Irish History* established his international reputation as a front-line thinker of the problems of emerging industrial societies.

In 1913 Connolly was in the thick of the labour disputes in Dublin which escalated into a general strike, called the Larkinite Strike after Larkin, who had called out all members of his ITGWU. The bitterness intensified

27

when Larkin took on the most formidable employer and opponent to the worker – William Martin Murphy, who owned, amongst many other businesses, a large multiple network of newsagents. Larkin urged all his members to stop handling Murphy's newspapers. After six months' appalling hardship the Dublin worker was defeated, but not cowed, when Murphy got the agreement of Dublin's other major employers to "lock out" their workers who belonged to Larkin's ITGWU. Massive street demonstrations clashed with the police in vicious brawls. Twice Larkin was locked up for seditious speeches and threatening to arm his workers – on one occasion haranguing the crowd disguised as a priest. In November 1913 the workers formed the Irish Citizen Army to protect their "locked-out" colleagues from the police and to provide a sense of cohesion and comradeship as the strikers began to falter.

Murphy was a Home-Ruler. Connolly lost no opportunity in pointing out to the workers that if Murphy supported Home Rule, then Home Rule could not be a good thing for the labour movement. Connolly deplored the partition of Ireland. He predicted, rightly, that the interests of Ulster's working man would became based on sectarian and not labour needs.

The strike failed and in 1914 Larkin went to America (he did not return to Ireland until 1923). When the Great War started Connolly was the driving force and unchallenged leader of the Irish labour movement, now officially organized as the Irish Labour Party, the ITGWU and the small Irish Citizen Army.

Connolly virulently opposed the Great War, which he saw as further evidence of capitalism exploiting the masses for its own self-indulgent aspirations of grabbing markets and colonies from the competitors. In his paper "Irish Worker" he urged the worker-masses of the combative nations to refuse to fight each other. To his great disappointment, patriotism, or, as Connolly argued, the exploitation and submissiveness of the masses, transcended his hope of a universal war-strike.

As the battalions of Europe clashed Connolly focused on Ireland's role in the war. In his paper he had satirized Redmond's appeal to the Irish Volunteers to fight in France:

Full steam ahead, John Redmond said
that everything was well, chum,
Home Rule will come when we are dead
and buried, out in Belgium.

Connolly defined his own attitude to the War:

I know of no foreign enemy in this country except the British Government. Should a German Army land in Ireland tomorrow, we should be perfectly justified in joining it, if by so doing we could rid this country once and for all of its connection with the Brigand Empire that drags us unwillingly to war.

By 1916 Connolly had to decide where his labour revolution stood with the numerous and exclusive nationalist movements. When Connolly agreed to join the Uprising, and was admitted to the I.R.B. military council in January 1916, he knew well enough the danger of his socialist movement becoming obliterated by a nationalist revolution dominated and directed by the middle-classes. He accepted the principle that for Ireland's special circumstances a political revolution was necessary as the first solution. But he was always explicit that at root

. . . . the struggle for Irish freedom has two aspects: it is national and it is social. The nationalist ideal can never be realised until Ireland stands forth before the world as a nation, free and independent. It is social and economic because no matter what the form of government may be, as long as one class owns the land and instrument of labour from which mankind derives their substance, that class will always have it in their power to plunder and enslave the remainder of their fellow creatures.

Of the Uprising's planners Pearse was nearest in sympathy to Connolly's socialist position. Pearse was not averse to a full nationalization programme but admitted "it was for the nation itself to determine the balance between public and private resources".

Connolly was painfully wounded in the foot in the Easter Uprising. During his brief captivity a surgeon, Richard Tobin, attended Connolly and has left us this account of his last days.

Tobin: "Can I do anything for you, Connolly?"
Connolly: "I want nothing but freedom."
"You must go elsewhere for that."
"What do you think will happen to me?"
"You'll be shot."
"Oh, you think that?"
"I am sure of it."
"Why?"
"They can't do anything else. Can they buy you?"
"No."

"Can they frighten you?"
"No."
"Will you promise if they let you off with your life to go away and be a good boy for the future?"
"No."
"They can do nothing else but shoot you."
"Oh. I recognise that."

When Connolly was brought to the place of execution, strapped to a chair because he was too weak to stand, the doctor asked him if he would pray for the men about to shoot him. Connolly smiled suddenly and radiantly on the firing squad: "I pray for all brave men who do their duty according to their lights."

Connolly is still little known outside Ireland. It is hard to see his brand of socialism, necessarily based on materialism, making much headway with a people invariably in thrall to their Catholic Church. Way back in 1910 Connolly had gently insisted, during a famous debate with the Jesuit priest Father Kane, that "socialism transcended religious differences". He was thinking not only of

Ulster Protestants but of religious and social conflicts everywhere. "Connolly", writes Leyland Lyons in *Ireland Since the Famine*, "was striking a note which, had he lived, might have had many reverberations."

Since his death some admirers have wanted Connolly canonized – though it's speculative whether Connolly himself would have liked the idea. His very sympathetic biographer, C. Desmond Greaves, in *The Life and Times of James Connolly* writes: "To canonize is to kill. He must be understood, estimated, and advanced from."

# David Lloyd George (1863-1945)

After the Easter Uprising was put down Asquith handed the Irish "problem" to David Lloyd George. Lloyd George knew he was taking a big risk with his political career. Success, however, would seal his position as the most brilliant and effective politician of his generation.

Lloyd George was born in England, where his father was a teacher. The family soon returned to Wales, their homeland. Lloyd George went into politics and, before long, he had acquired the reputation of being the peoples' politician – a man who fought for the rights of defenceless groups and suppressed nations. As Chancellor of the Exchequer (1908-15) Lloyd George showed all his brilliance, tenacity and fearlessness when he launched his Peoples' Budget: "a war budget," he said, "to wage warfare against poverty and squalidness". His opponents, especially the Tory land-owning peers whose land was to be taxed for the first time, called his Budget "unfair, unjust, oppressive, unequal", and harassed Lloyd George all the way. Lloyd George retaliated in powerful, witty speeches which showed he was quite prepared to take on the establishment though many of his Liberal colleagues dared not to. His speech on 9 October 1910 at Newcastle-on-Tyne, where many listeners were unemployed, was one of his most virtuoso:

As long as they [peers] preserved their stately silence which became their rank and their intelligence, all went well. They have been scolding because the Budget cart has knocked a little of the gilt off their old stage coach. . . . Let them realise what they are doing . . . issues will be raised which they little dream of. One question will be asked: whether 500 men [the peers], ordinary men chosen accidently from among the unemployed, should override the judgement of millions of people who are engaged in the industry which makes the wealth of the country. That is one question. Another will be: who ordained that a few should have the land of Britain as a pre-requisite? Who made ten thousand people owners of the soil, and the rest of us trespassers in the land of our birth?

Recalling this kind of sympathy and political thrust, many people were surprised that Lloyd George offered the suppressed Irish no more in 1916 than Asquith did in 1914. The truth was that Lloyd George was more of an imperialist than might be thought. He had opposed the Boer War (1899) because he believed British policy was unjust and foolish, not because he was a pacifist or against imperialism. His imperialism was based on equality among nations. He was a life Home-Ruler, but always resisted any national movement which would fragment the Empire. In Belfast in 1907 Lloyd George had said:

To sever the bonds – why, it would be a loss to

Ireland. It would be a greater loss to the Empire. The greatest loss would be to Humanity, if you confine the brilliant genius of Ireland within the bounds of an island, when you have hundreds of millions of the human race who would be benefited by your taking a full share in the direction of the British Empire.

Moreover, during his premiership Lloyd George's policies were constrained by being the leader of coalition governments, which included the most inflexible Conservative/Unionists. In 1918 he complained:

I have to make compromises all the time in order to conciliate different sections. . . . Take the Irish question. If I had a clear majority in the House of Commons I could soon settle it.

In 1916 an Irish solution was particularly urgent if America was to be united behind the Allied war effort. Nothing embarrassed Asquith's Government more than the Uprising's aim to free a small nation – the very principle on which England had declared war against Germany and which, it was hoped, would bring America into the war. Lloyd George told Carson:

In six months the War will be lost. . . . The Irish-American vote will go over to the German side . . . unless something is done, even provisionally, to satisfy America.

Lloyd George's scheme was provisional; he promised a more enduring settlement after the war. For the moment he had to quieten Ireland, pacify American opinion and reassure the Unionists. By mid-June Lloyd George placed his plan before the Cabinet: Home Rule to be effective at once for 26 of the 32 counties. To resolve the contentious issue of the six counties of North-East Ulster Lloyd George deviously told Carson and Redmond what each wanted to hear – Redmond that Ulster's exclusion was temporary and Carson:

We must make it clear at the end of the provisional period Ulster does not merge in the rest of Ireland.

As in 1914, the proposal foundered because hard-line Unionist ministers and peers insisted that Ulster's exclusion be permanent and explicitly stated as such. In addition the southern Unionists were, said Lloyd George, "moving heaven and the other place to thwart settlement". Any lingering hopes that talks might revive were dashed when, in July, Lloyd George's contradictory promises to Redmond and Carson were disclosed. His letter of resignation was endorsed "Not Sent".

The historian, George Boyce, wrote:

Lloyd George knew that he was not yet politically indispensable, and he was resolved not to suffer the fate of other British statesmen who had faced, and failed to solve, the Irish question. However we may judge his conduct . . . he was well advised to sacrifice his Irish settlement and live to fight another day: for in six months he was to become prime minister. (*Lloyd George: Twelve Essays*)

In 1918 Lloyd George was confronted with the Irish Conscription issue. After the German offensive in March powerful Conservatives insisted that Ireland should accept conscription. Up to then Lloyd George had

**25** Irish conscription became a burning issue as the Great War casualties mounted.

opposed conscription. Now, he wrote to C.P. Scott, Editor of the *Manchester Guardian*, "Conscription was a political necessity if the Tories were to accept Home Rule." He urged the Tories to concede Home Rule provided Ireland accepted conscription. Expanding his argument he said if Ireland resisted conscription the Irish were not worthy of the responsibilities for Home Rule. This argument showed Lloyd George at his most politically imaginative because pressure was also on the Tories to show they could place honour and reason above sectarian interests. But this ingenious proposal had been overtaken by events in Ireland. Home Rule was now irrelevant, because Ireland was moving rapidly to republican Sinn Féin and conscription would have been opposed with "red war".

The 1918 General Election which brought Sinn Féin to power also returned Lloyd George to power as Prime Minister of a Tory-dominated coalition government. This was the precarious framework within which Lloyd George had to work for an Irish settlement, with a secessionist government in Dublin which was soon to be at war with England.

**27**  Lloyd George (left), like many politicians, found de Valera inscrutable.

**26**  Women protesting against England's executions during the Anglo-Irish War, 1921.

When the truce of 1921 suspended two and a half years of grim fighting Lloyd George had finally decided that the key to the Irish solution existed in England. Only when Ulster and the Unionist lobby had been gratified could terms be explored for Nationalist Ireland.

By 1919 Ulster had accepted the inevitability of Home Rule and was prepared to "do business" on the basis of the six Protestant-dominated Ulster counties staying out of the rest of Ireland, remaining closely linked with the U.K. and having their own local Parliament in Belfast. In 1920 such an arrangement was agreed with Ulster. For Southern Ireland, Lloyd George accepted the opinion of his advisers in Dublin that Sinn

Féin might be attracted to talks on a basis of reaching a Dominion-status settlement, as with Canada and South Africa.

Lloyd George handled the two intractable issues of partition and Irish sovereignty in masterly fashion. Lloyd George won Arthur Griffith's agreement to the Boundary Clause principle (page 12), which pointed the way to future Irish unity. For weeks the negotiators haggled on the wording which constitutionally linked Ireland with England. Worn out, and worn down, by Lloyd George's impatience and threats to renew the war, the Southern Irish signed the Anglo-Irish Treaty with grave misgivings.

Lloyd George seemed to have achieved a minor miracle. He had got Irish Unionists and Nationalists to accept a settlement that neither at heart wanted, and the Government to support a solution which seven years before would have been contemptuously rejected. However, as civil war tore Ireland apart, and when de Valera began to dismantle the Treaty from 1932 onwards, Lloyd George's achievement seemed flawed.

The retention of Ireland in the Empire was nominally achieved, but at the expense of reality. (Robert Rhodes James, *The British Revolution*, Vol. 2)

THE KINDEST CUT OF ALL.

Welsh Wizard. "I NOW PROCEED TO CUT THIS MAP INTO TWO PARTS AND PLACE THEM IN THE HAT. AFTER A SUITABLE INTERVAL THEY WILL BE FOUND TO HAVE COME TOGETHER OF THEIR OWN ACCORD—(ASIDE)—AT LEAST LET'S HOPE SO, I'VE NEVER DONE THIS TRICK BEFORE."

**28** Lloyd George's Home Rule Bill is satirized by Punch, 10 March 1920.

# Michael Collins (1890-1922)

On 25 September 1917 a Volunteer called Thomas Ashe died in prison from ill-treatment. Ashe's funeral became the occasion for a massive political demonstration, in every way as spectacular as Rossa's (page 23) and, like Rossa's, was organized by the I.R.B. Nine thousand Volunteers, carrying their rifles reversed, and 30,000 civilians were present. The English had forbidden all gatherings but the security forces dared not interfere: The *Daily Express* wrote that Ashe's death and funeral had made "100,000 Sinn Féiners out of 100,000 constitutional Nationalists". After a volley was fired over the grave a young man, 27 years old, in Volunteers' uniform, stepped forward and spoke one sentence: "The volley we have just heard is the only speech which it is proper to make over the grave of a dead Fenian." The man was Michael Collins.

Never a man for long speeches, even when a

**29** Michael Collins led the resistance to England's occupation of Ireland. His brilliant tactics and commanding presence inspired the Irish and dispirited the English.

from the Gaelic League and returned to Dublin in 1916 to take part in the Uprising. He was Joseph Plunkett's aide-de-camp and impressed everyone as "the most active and efficient officer in the place [G.P.O.]". Collins was never sentimental about the Uprising. He believed the High Command was inept, especially in its choice of positions to defend. During the "Troubles" a friend walking with Collins past the G.P.O. nostalgically recalled the "good fight". "No, it was not," retorted Collins tersely, "We lost".

Desmond Ryan, the celebrated writer on early Fenian history wrote:

There were two Micks, one the jolly, hard-swearing, good fellow; the other a dour, quiet man who lived with his life in his hand, heroic, dignified, a thinker, a fighter, a mystery. (*Remembering Sion*)

Collins was a big, athletic man with a huge capacity for work and an incisive mind which reached quickly to the root of a problem. Many loved and admired him for these qualities but Collins was intolerant of those who failed to match his exacting standards. Dan Breen, a born fighter who shot down the two policemen in January 1914 and precipitated the Anglo-Irish War, said he would willingly lay down his life for Collins, but admitted that Collins "would never give you a second chance". According to the historian Leyland Lyons, in *Ireland Since the Famine*, most striking of all about Collins was "the political realist, the ruthless conspirator who had no time for high-flown sentiment or romantic idealism".

Collins was not one to languish in a prison camp. In Frongoch he subverted camp regulations and, most significant for the future, he established an I.R.B. group among the internees. The group was divided into cells and members of each cell came from the same region in Ireland. When the Volunteers were released Collins already had a network of national resistance once the War of Independence started.

Late in 1916 Collins was released. His organizational ability and his I.R.B.

minister in the Dáil, Collins was master of the short, telling statement. Collins is best known for masterminding the subversive campaign in the Anglo-Irish War. His skill and flair in guerilla operations inspired similar freedom-fighting movements after the Second World War. Thomas Jones, deputy-secretary to Lloyd George's Cabinet, echoed many Englishmen's thoughts when he wrote in his diary: "Where was Michael Collins during the Great War? One of him is worth ten brass-hats [generals]."

For part of the war Collins was among many Volunteers interned in Frongoch camp after the Uprising. He had escaped execution because he had no police record.

Michael Collins was born in County Cork. He left school at 16 and worked at clerical jobs in London. In 1909 he graduated to the I.R.B.

connections were largely responsible for the important Sinn Féin victory in the Roscommon by-election (page 10). When Field Marshal Sir John French was sent to pacify Ireland during the Irish Conscription Crisis of 1917 Collins' intelligence system was so tight that he alone of leading Sinn Féiners escaped arrest.

The assassination of the two policemen by Dan Breen shocked many Irish people who had hoped England would adopt a "live and let live" policy towards the "rebel" Sinn Féin government. But Collins told an uneasy Sinn Féin executive:

The sooner the fighting is forced and a general state of disorder created throughout the country, the better it will be for the country.

During the Anglo-Irish War Collins led a double life. By day he was the Minister for Finance, one of whose achievements was to raise a huge loan to help the investment programme of the new republican government (the most intelligent English investigators never traced this fund); by night Collins directed the grim work of his assassination "squad" with the purpose of, in Collins' graphic words, "putting out the eyes of the British".

During the war the Sinn Féin government was quite unable to meet regularly. Affairs of State were discussed on the run from the police in "safe houses". Collins' intelligence network was so efficient that he walked openly the streets of Dublin. He was never caught, though British Security searched for him incessantly. Typical of Collins' coolness, and an indication of his efficient network, was an incident that happened one night when walking with a friend. Much to his friend's consternation Collins led the way to the H.Q. of the Dublin Metropolitan Police. The duty policeman was Sergeant Broy, who shortly before had met Collins and knew at once "he was the man who could beat the British and I decided to work for him from then on". Broy led Collins to the top security file, where he

**30** Collins' Assassination Squad terrorized the Royal Irish Constabulary.

**31** The "Black and Tans" were tough ex-servicemen, recruited in England, who operated in support of the Royal Irish Constabulary.

**32** Refugees leaving Balbriggan. Their work places and homes had been destroyed by the "Tans" in a calculated policy of ruining the social and economic base of communities.

spent seven hours extricating all the information on Sinn Féin, including himself, and the names of Irish informers and British agents. These informers and agents were subsequently warned to leave their jobs, or take the consequences.

Collins' execution "squad" numbered 12 leaders – the Twelve Apostles they were called. Some, like Charlie Dalton, were drawn from the upper-middle-class and others, like Bill Stapleton, from the labourer and office worker groups. By January 1920, 34 R.I.C. security officers had been killed or wounded. The R.I.C. was cowed and recruitment fell alarmingly. The tough and brilliant Detective-Inspector Redmond was sent down from Belfast to arrest Collins. Within weeks he was marked down and shot. These were the circumstances which saw the deployment in Ireland of the notorious "Black and Tans" (page 11).

By Spring 1921 Lloyd George exclaimed: "We have murder by the throat." Collins privately wondered how many more weeks Ireland could hold out. He knew, though, that for every day he did hold out England was losing moral credit with a critical world audience. So, when a truce was declared on 21 July, Collins could confidently say:

World opinion has forced the British to take the step of having these conferences with us. They want to clear their name with the world.

Never was the political realism of Collins more evident than in his reaction to the Treaty terms, which he was first to sign. He accepted that England had given far more than she would have liked. The Treaty was signed at 2.10 a.m. on 6 December. Afterwards, a dispirited Collins paced the lonely London streets. Perceptively, he reflected on the consequences of the agreement.

When you have sweated, toiled, had mad dreams, hopeless nightmares, you find yourself in London's streets cold and dank in the night air. Think – what I have got for Ireland? Something which she has wanted these past seven hundred years. Will anyone be satisfied at the bargain? Will anyone? I tell you this – early this morning I signed my death warrant.

In a memorable phrase Collins told the Dáil that the Irish delegation had brought back "not the ultimate freedom that all nations aspire and develop to, but the freedom to achieve it".

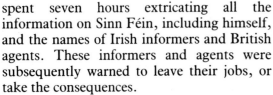

**33** The Irish peace delegation in London. Collins is ▶ at the table in the centre, with Childers standing behind. Griffith is seated on the left.

Collins tried desperately to avert civil war. He could count on the loyalty of many old comrades in the I.R.A. But to hard-line I.R.A. groups the settlement was a sell-out. The I.R.A. split into two factions, the pro-Treaty and the anti-Treaty I.R.A. (known as the "Irregulars").

In spite of the summer General Election which actually increased the pro-Treaty T.D.s from 64 to 94, the civil war intensified. At 7.30 p.m. on 22 August 1922 Collins was travelling in a convoy in County Cork – safe country, he thought, where he was born and no one would harm him. Half-an-hour later he was dead. The convoy had fallen into an ambush. Recklessly, but characteristically, Collins had gone forward to join the fight. He was hit in the back of the head by a ricochet bullet right at the end of the battle. His last words were, "Forgive them". Within ten days the Irish Free State had lost her President (Griffith) and now her Prime Minister and Commander-in-Chief. But the Government forces were winning the war. Massive recruitment drives, and weapons from England, had squeezed the "Irregulars" into small pockets of resistance in the Deep South.

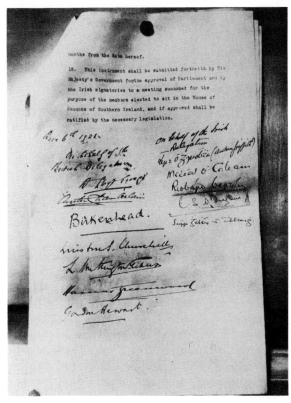

**34** The signatories to the Anglo-Irish Treaty, 6 December 1921. Notice the Irish names (right) are in Gaelic.

# Eamon de Valera (1882-1975)

Eamon de Valera escaped execution after the Uprising almost by chance. His American connection on his father's side may have helped save his life. Also, by the time de Valera's trial came up, public opinion had become repelled by the shootings.

De Valera was born in New York. His father died when he was two years old and his widowed mother sent him to Ireland, where his grandmother brought him up in a labourer's cottage. De Valera won a scholarship to Blackrock College, Dublin, and in 1904 he graduated in Maths from the Royal University. By 1906 he was a professor of Mathematics. He joined the Gaelic League and remained devoted to the Gaelic language all his life. He was among the first to join the Volunteers and trained himself by persistence to become a competent, reliable and humane officer.

Irish nationalism was a duty, not a passion, for de Valera. He joined the I.R.B. but never attended meetings. During the Uprising he commanded the detachment at Boland's Bakery. This was the most important military position because it covered the road from Dublin harbour along which English reinforcements had to advance. Here the English suffered their severest casualties before de Valera was ordered to surrender. He said to the English officer, "Shoot me if you will but arrange for my men." As he marched off to captivity at the head of his men he murmured to a gathering crowd, "Oh, if you'd only come out with knives and forks."

The authority of de Valera emerged in the prison camps. His firm but sensitive discipline sustained the morale of the other Volunteers. When de Valera was released in 1917 he had already attracted a devoted following. People also looked to him for political direction because he was the senior surviving commander of Easter 1916. In the late summer of 1917 de Valera's chance came when he contested East Clare. East Clare is an historic election for two reasons. It was de Valera's first political challenge. Also, the country was riveted, for de Valera took his stand on Patrick Pearse's republican principles which he had declared on the G.P.O. steps in 1916. Here was the moment when the Irish would decide whether the Uprising had any meaning in practical terms beyond the emotion of Pearse's speeches, the power of Yeats' poetry and beyond the revulsion felt at the execution of the patriots. De Valera won a crushing victory, polling over twice as many votes as his opponent, Patrick Lynch K.C., the Irish Nationalist nominee. The result was a renunciation of Home Rule and a call for the political aims of the 1916 revolutionaries.

Throughout the election campaign de Valera's attitude was consistently reflected in his words:

We want an Irish republic. . . . But if the Irish

**35** After the Uprising de Valera was among hundreds interned.

people wanted to have another form of government, so long as it was an Irish government, I would not put in a word against it.

These words tell us quite a lot about de Valera's political personality. While it is clear what kind of government de Valera wanted he was keeping his options open. The reasonableness of his message may have impressed a lot of Irish who were disillusioned Home Rulers but were wary of extremism. People often found de Valera's opinions elusive during his long political life. He never liked to commit himself until the last moment or until he had extracted all the information from a protagonist. People said that "grappling with de Valera's thoughts is like trying to pick up mercury with a fork". Men of affairs like Lloyd George became exasperated with de Valera's meticulous, labyrinthine approach even to a simple problem.

Before East Clare de Valera was a remote figure. He possessed none of the fiery nationalism of Pearse or the prestige of Griffith and MacNeill. He was austere, not easy to know: a man who projected his ideas intellectually rather than as a political activist. Nevertheless, his success at East Clare resulted in nationalist Ireland looking to de Valera as the new nationalist leader – the man who could speak for Republicans without frightening off moderate Nationalists.

At the famous convention that autumn Sinn Féin and the I.R.B. agreed to unite under one organization and one leader. Arthur Griffith stood down as President of Sinn Féin in favour of de Valera, saying:

Since Parnell's day there was not a man to equal de Valera and I am sure in following him and standing by him loyally we should bring the Irish cause to the goal for which many Irishmen in hopeful generations suffered.

During the Irish Conscription Crisis de Valera was arrested and imprisoned in Lincoln jail. There, he heard the news that Sinn Féin had won a landslide victory in the 1918 General Election (December). In February 1919 de Valera was daringly rescued

**36** In his 1918-20 tour of America de Valera won much sympathy but failed to obtain the crucial presidential backing for the new Irish State.

by Collins. Two months later de Valera was unanimously elected President (Prime Minister) of the "rebel" Sinn Féin government.

De Valera had to win foreign, especially American, recognition if the insecure Irish Republic were to survive England's opposition. From June 1919 to December 1920 de Valera was in America. He negotiated a $6 million loan (a huge amount in those days) to sustain the Republic. He won wide popular sympathy but he failed to win the crucial presidential backing for the new Irish state. During his absence, Griffith deputized for him until his arrest: then Collins took over. De Valera returned to Ireland (1920) to find the Anglo-Irish War at its grimest, and the "Black and Tans" creating havoc. At first there seemed no common ground on which de Valera, the Republican, and Lloyd George, the Home-Ruler, could open negotiations. However, the chance for talks was seized when de Valera told the T.D.s that the new Dáil "had been a vote for a freedom and independence rather than for a particular form of government because we are not republican doctrinaires". To Lloyd George de Valera wrote that Ireland sought "a certain treaty and free association with the British

Commonwealth". That de Valera seemed prepared to negotiate on terms that would allow for some sort of relationship with the British government was sufficient to allow peace talks to begin.

Many people were surprised that de Valera did not attend the peace talks. Possibly he wanted to distance himself from a treaty which he felt all along would fail to provide the only kind of complete independence he really wanted for Ireland. De Valera voted against the Treaty in the Dáil's debate. He repeated the well-worn anti-Treaty argument: "The Treaty gives away Irish independence; it brings us into the British Empire". When the T.D.s voted by seven for the Treaty de Valera resigned. In the Civil War that followed he enlisted as a private in his old Uprising unit and appealed for public support from "the men who had refused to forswear their allegiance to the Republic". When the "War of the Brothers" ended de Valera's political fortunes had reached rock bottom. He consistently attacked the Treaty and spent a year in prison for his opposition.

The rest of de Valera's political life, though outside the years covered by this book, is a consequence of the Anglo-Irish Treaty. In

**37** De Valera denounces the Peace Treaty and appeals for support at an anti-Treaty meeting, February 1922. Civil war followed.

1927 he founded a new party called Fianna Fáil, which won 44 of the 155 seats in its first General Election that year. His party would not sit in the Dáil because it refused to sign the Oath of Allegiance which the Treaty demanded. But, recognizing the futility of denying nearly one-third of the electorate representation in the Dáil, de Valera agreed to sign the Oath. The gesture was meaningless because de Valera instructed his party not to read what they were signing! In 1932 de Valera formed his first government and remained in power until 1948. Stealthily, he proceeded to dismantle all aspects of the 1921 Treaty which linked Ireland with England. By 1938 Southern Ireland was truly republican with not an English ship in an Irish port or an English soldier on Irish soil unless invited.

When de Valera died, aged 93, he enjoyed a worldwide authority, "unequalled by an Irish leader since the fall of Parnell nearly 90 years before". In spite of many achievements his failure to unite Ireland flawed his life's work and clouded his last years.

# WRITERS

The Easter Uprising generation produced a revival of Irish writing so remarkable that it became known as the Irish Literary Renaissance. With the notable exception of Sean O'Casey most were well-to-do Anglo-Irish.

The writers' problem was to come to terms with the new thrust of nationalism and to find their own role in it. The direction which the writers took was not popular with the Irish. W.P. Ryan, an Irish journalist, argued: "We are working for a new Irish civilisation, quite distinct from the English . . . without our own [civilisation] we may be but cultured slaves." W.B. Yeats retorted that Irish writers had the opportunity of uniting "The First Born of the Coming Race, a composite of Anglo-Irish and Gaelic-Irish, Catholic and Protestant, North and South". Nor would Yeats abnegate the writer's art – "a criticism of life", he often said – to a national diktat. Standing on this principle Yeats and Sean O'Casey were alienated from nationalist Ireland for some years. Yeats and O'Casey were maligned by Irish audiences because they refused to treat their characters sentimentally or, always, patriotically. In those day of feverish nationalism it was not easy for every Irish person to see that the failings and frailties of Yeats' peasant and O'Casey's labourer made the characters far more sympathetic than if they had been moulded into flawless immortals.

Easter 1916 was the crucial watershed in the life of Yeats and his fellow writers.

## W.B. Yeats (1865-1939)

William Yeats was in England when reports of the Easter Uprising reached him. A few years before he had left Ireland, disillusioned with "this bitter, blind land".

In the same way as for most people, the Uprising took him completely by surprise. He was also annoyed, because he was the leading, and most contentious, figure in the literary nationalism of Ireland and expected to be informed of plans for a political revolution. As he travelled back to Ireland he was overcome with remorse. He had failed to gauge the determination of the revolutionaries. He used to meet Pearse, and other revolutionaries, hear of their fantasies for a free Ireland and, secretly, despise them as ineffectual dreamers.

Yeats wandered gloomily among those hallowed places in central Dublin where the revolutionaries had defied England for a week and allowed the occasion and its meaning to soak into his bloodstream. And then Yeats wrote one of his memorable poems which, perhaps as much as anything or anyone else, changed Irish opinion from condemnation to an understanding of the revolutionaries.

Until 1914 Yeats' poetry had been elaborate – too "mysterious and inscrutable" to reach a popular audience. The subjects were either obscure Celtic legends or rather sad reflections on his unrequited love for the actress Maud Gonne. Now Yeats wrote a poem which deeply affected Irish people by its power and

**38** William Yeats led the revival of Irish literature. Nationalists maligned Yeats because he wouldn't idealize the Irish. He also insisted on writing poems and producing plays in English.

beauty – beauty to move people to tears and power to drive people to action. The poem was called "The Rose Tree". The rose is a sacred symbol to Ireland, invoked by many other Irish poets. Ireland's national colour, green, is also used in a clever, symbolic way.

"O words are lightly spoken."
Said Pearse to Connolly,
"May be a breath of politic words
Has withered our Rose Tree;
Or maybe but a wind that blows
Across the bitter sea."

"It needs to be but watered."
James Connolly replied,
"To make the green come out again
And spread on every side.
And shake the blossom from the bud
To be the garden's pride."

"But where can we draw water,"
Said Pearse to Connolly,
"When all the wells are parched away?"
"O plain as plain can be.
There's nothing but our own red blood
Can make a right Rose Tree."

The apathy of Ireland, the resolution of the insurgents and the sense of guilt pervade the poem; and in the last two lines of "Easter 1916" Yeats predicted the awesome and glorious consequences of the Uprising:

All changed, changed utterly:
A terrible beauty is born.

But it took some years before Yeats achieved wide sympathy.

William Yeats was the son of an Anglican clergyman whose family settled in Ireland at the end of the seventeenth century. Yeats was educated at the Godolphin School in West London and studied Law and Art in Dublin before turning to literature. His first poetry, written when a teenager, very much imitated Shelley, Spenser and Blake. Once Yeats had found the writer's role he directed his energy to creating a national consciousness by adapting old Irish stories for contemporary audiences. He was also active in establishing Irish literary societies in London and Dublin, and with Lady Gregory and John Synge he founded the famous Abbey Theatre. This "small, dingy and impecunious" house marked the "launching of a dramatic movement which made Dublin an important literary capital in the first quarter of the century". There, Yeats produced plays on Irish people by Irish doctors, soldiers, teachers, labourers as well as by established writers. For a while he was a member of the I.R.B. though his heart wasn't totally absorbed by narrow extreme republicanism.

Before long Yeats produced two plays at the Abbey which provoked a storm of rage. His own play, *The Countess Cathleen*, was about

**39** The Abbey Theatre, founded by Yeats and where ▶ he produced some contentious plays.

two devils who came to Ireland and tempted the peasants to sell their souls for gold. In the end the Countess sacrifices her possessions and her soul for the peasants. Catholic nationalist opinion was repelled by the slur on the morals of Irish people. The second play was Synge's *In the Shadow of the Glen*, which portrayed the loneliness and frustration of a young peasant woman married to an old man. She elopes with a passing "tramp". Griffith led the widespread denunciation;

A lie, because all of us know that Irish women are the most virtuous in the world, and in no country are women so faithful to the marriage bond as in Ireland.

From all sides the basic argument was repeated that an artist must subordinate aesthetic effects to the national cause. Yeats naturally argued the reverse – that truth in art cannot exist if it is muzzled by national constraints. Most cutting of all was Maude Gonne:

Mr Yeats asks for freedom for the theatre, freedom even from patriotic captivity. I would

40   Yeats was in love with Maud Gonne for most of his life. Maud was the daughter of a British officer. She married the revolutionary John McBride who was shot after the Uprising. Maud outraged her class by exposing English atrocities in Ireland to the French and, accompanied by James Connolly, appeared bearing a black coffin in the wake of Queen Victoria's jubilee procession in Dublin (1900).

ask for freedom for it from one thing more deadly than all else – freedom from the insidious and destructive tyranny of foreign influence.

All his life Yeats remained devoted to the talented, entrancing Maud Gonne, described by W. Stead, the editor of *The Times*, who met her in St Petersburg, as "the most beautiful woman in Europe". Yeats met her in 1889 since when "all the trouble of my life began".

When Yeats told Maud he couldn't be happy without her, she told him;

Oh yes you can, because you make beautiful poetry out of what you call your unhappiness, and you are happy in that.

Yeats wrote his play *Cathleen ni Houlihan* (1903) in honour of Maud, who took the title part – a woman who symbolized Ireland for

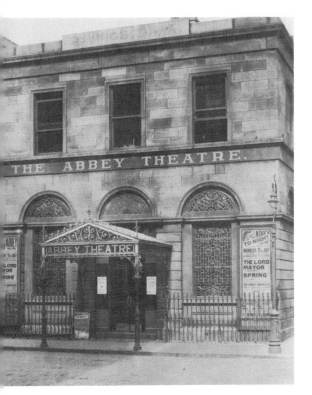

whom people will die. This was much more in the spirit of the times though one person wondered whether such a play should be shown "unless one was prepared to go out to shoot and be shot". Yeats was disturbed by this reaction and in old age still asked: "Did that play of mine send out certain men to be shot?" Eventually, in 1917, he married an old friend, Georgie Hyde-Lees, and his life became "serene and full of order".

Though he did not actually return to live permanently in Ireland until 1922 he involved himself more with Irish affairs after 1916. In October 1918 Yeats wrote from Dublin on Irish conscription to Lord Haldene, recently Lord Chancellor and a former Minister for War:

I am alarmed at the state of feeling. . . . Lady Gregory [a close friend] who knows the country as few know it is convinced that the women and children will stand in front of their men and receive the bullets. It seems to me a strangely wanton thing that England, for the sake of 50,000 Irish soldiers is prepared to hollow another trench between the countries and fill it with blood.

From 1916 Yeats' poetry grew in authority. Supported by a happy, contented married life he took more part in public life. His most sustained creative period was 1919-33, which included *The Wild Swan at Coole* (1919) and *The Winding Stair* (1933). His themes are friends, political upheaval in Ireland and a search for the values of life. In 1922 he went to live in a ruined Norman castle in Galway, which he had bought in 1915. Thoor Ballylee was close to Lady Gregory's Coole Park where, a quarter of a century before, he made his first visit in low spirits and left revitalized. That year, Prime Minister William Cosgrave appointed him to the Senate of the Irish Free State in recognition of his services to Ireland, and, in 1923, the world recognized his influence when he was awarded the Nobel Prize for Literature.

Yeats is universally acclaimed as the greatest poet of his age. More than that, at Easter 1916 he found the inspiration to bring him close to the very people for whose freedom he had fought in his own independent way and whom he very nearly lost. T.S. Eliot said that Yeats was

. . . one of those few poets whose history is the history of our own time, who are a part of the consciousness of their age, which cannot be understood without them.

**41** Yeats wrote some plays for Maud. Here, she (centre) plays the main character in *The Countess Cathleen.*

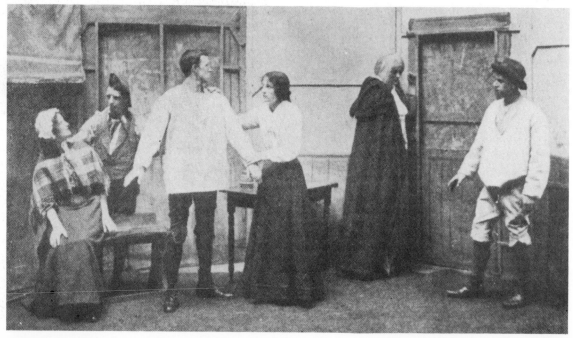

# Sean O'Casey (1880-1964)

One day in April 1923 Gabriel Fallon, then an actor with the Abbey Theatre in Dublin (later a director), overheard a dress rehearsal of a new play. The play was *The Shadow of the Gunman*, by "a chap called O'Casey, a Dublin labourer". The play was only on for three nights, "to let the poor fellow see how bad it was", Fallon was told by Augusta, Lady Gregory. In time, Lady Gregory became very impressed with O'Casey plays, recording in her journal that *Juno and the Paycock* was "a wonderful and terrible [terrifying] play of futility, of irony, humour and tragedy"; and that *The Plough and the Stars* was "an overpowering play . . . all others would seem so shadowy".

Other people were not so impressed. O'Casey's characters are not heroic – the women mostly are strong, positive, sometimes noble and sympathetic but not nationalistic-minded; the men are vain, self-centred, usually weak – dreamers whose illusions bring adversity or death to their women. Moreover, O'Casey's attitudes angered many Irish. In *The Shadow of the Gunman* Seumas Shields says:

I believe in the freedom of Ireland, an' that England has no right to be here, but I draw the line when I hear the gunmen blowin' about dyin' for the people, when it's the people that are dyin' for the gunmen!

The Shields of O'Casey's world would not have been out in Dublin streets during Easter week 1916. Dublin audiences were outraged at such a defamatory view of the Uprising and the Irish War of Independence, which were hallowed occasions and form an essential part of modern Irish legend.

These unheroic currents prevailed in the third of O'Casey's three masterpieces, *The Plough and the Stars*. The President of the Gaelic League "had to leave before the Second Act from a fit of nausea", and he missed the scene when snatches of Patrick Pearse's most stirring speeches are greeted with scorn by people to whom political freedom was meaningless and "economic freedom" everything. The spirited Rosie speaks for others when she says: "They're not goin' to get Rosie Redmond, says I, to fight for freedom that wouldn't be worth winnin' in a raffle!" Some Abbey actors and directors objected to other lines and actions. The audience jeered and rioted when Yeats bravely tried to speak from the stage. O'Casey was surrounded in the foyer and abused and the police were called in.

**42** Sean O'Casey refused to treat the characters in his plays sentimentally.

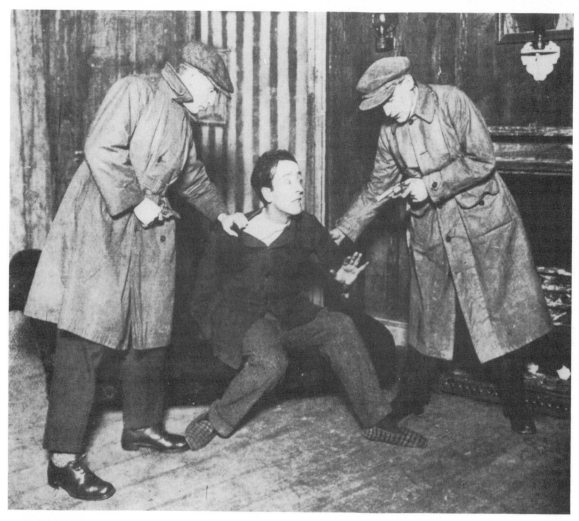

During the rehearsal of *Juno and the Paycock* the producers cut out part of a disturbing scene which, nevertheless, was essential to O'Casey's realism. In this sequence Johnny Boyle, who was wounded fighting first the English in the Uprising and then the Free State government, is now suspected of betraying an anti-Treaty I.R.A. comrade (Tancred) to the Government forces. Two sinister "Irregulars" have called on Johnny in his tenement home and warned him to attend an interrogation:

Johnny: I'm not goin', then. I know nothing about Tancred.
Irregular: You'd better come for your own sake – remember your oath.
Johnny: (passionately) I won't go! Haven't I done enough for Ireland! I've lost me arm, an me hip's destroyed so that I'll never be able to walk right agen! Good God, haven't I done enough for Ireland?
Irregular: Boyle, no man can do enough for Ireland!

The characters in O'Casey's plays represented attitudes and a lifestyle with which he was very familiar. They may have been alien to, and remote from, the high ideals and lofty aims of Griffith's and Pearse's world. None the less, the brutalizing world O'Casey wrote about was just as real – the world of Connolly's socialism.

Sean O'Casey was a child of Dublin's slum tenements, the youngest of 13 children of whom eight died in infancy. He was born, and

**43 and 44** Tense moments in O'Casey plays: (left) in *Juno and the Paycock*, set in The Irish Civil War, two anti-Treaty rebels are taking away a suspected informer for execution; (right) a scene from *The Plough and the Stars*, set in the Easter Uprising. Nora Clitheroe pleads with her husband not to fight.

O'Casey was drawn into the labour movement by Larkin and helped set up the Irish Labour Party. He was soon sworn into the I.R.B. by Tom Clarke. During the 1913 "lock-out" strikes O'Casey was section leader in the Irish Citizen Army (see p.28) and later wrote its history. Speaking of Larkin's vision of a secure society with time to enjoy the beauty of life O'Casey said, "Here was a man who would put a flower in a vase on a table as well as a loaf on a table."

O'Casey never participated in the Easter Uprising. He asserted that the leaders of the Irish Volunteers had not the interest of the workers at heart. He bitterly resented Connolly bringing out the Citizen Army in an irrelevant revolt. During the Rising he roamed the streets and left this vivid writer's account of the destruction of the G.P.O.

In the sky the flames were soaring higher, till the heavens looked like a great ruby hanging from God's ear. Now it was above them [Volunteers] locking away the roof from over their heads, and they were too weary to go on trying to put it out. Their faces were chipped into bleeding jaggedness by splinters flying from shattered stones and brick . . . their leaders, before a wall of flame, standing dignified among them, already garlanded for death. They had helped God to rouse up Ireland.

O'Casey's embattled time with Ireland and the Abbey led to his self-imposed exile in 1926, a year after he had decided to write full time. He had alienated many sectors of Irish society. Still more were enraged when O'Casey wrote in his history of the Citizen Army that the real hero of Easter 1916 was none of the executed patriots but the pacifist Francis Sheehy-Skeffington (page 9).

The Church also was very hostile to O'Casey. O'Casey's communism was a result of the inability of either Church or established political systems to overcome, or care about, the misery and inhumanity of man. O'Casey satirized the Church's manipulation of Christianity and her exaltation of man's humility while seeming blind to the humiliation of man in his destitution. "Didn't

for many years lived, in dire poverty and under severe physical hardship. He was nearly blind and usually wore a peaked cap to protect his inflamed, diseased eyes from glare. He picked up any labouring or dock job which came his way. Though he worked a 13-hour day he still had the energy to attend Gaelic League meetings in the evening. A contemporary remembers O'Casey at this time:

A tall, short-sighted man with an intelligent, sardonic face. Neck and throat bound in the coils of a white muffler, a Jacobin [revolutionary] of Jacobins, as his small red-rimmed eyes stab all the beauty and sorrow of the world in bursts of anti-English rhetoric.

they [the priests] prevent the people in '47 from seizin' the corn, an' they starvin?" asks Captain Boyle in *Juno and the Paycock*. "Didn't they down Parnell; didn't they say that hell wasn't hot enough nor eternity long enough to punish the Fenians?" Yet the poignant last scene in *Juno* reflects a belief, or hope, in the idea of God. The Boyle family is disintegrating as one savage misfortune follows another – the hopeless father is drunk, down to his last penny of borrowed money, mutters incoherently, lost to his fantasy world; the bailiffs are taking away the Boyles' possessions; two policemen call asking the Boyle parents to identify the body of a shot man who is their son Johnny; and Mary, the unmarried daughter, announces she is pregnant. Juno tries to calm her hysterical daughter:

Mary: . . . there isn't a God; if there were He wouldn't let these things happen!
Juno: Mary, you mustn't say them things. We'll want all the help we can get from God an' His Blessed Mother now! These things have nothin' to do with the Will of God. Ah, what can God do agen the stupidity o' men!

And when Juno first hears of her son's death she says,

. . . Sacred Heart o' Jesus, take away our hearts o' stone and give us our hearts o' flesh. Take away this murdherin' hate and give us thine eternal love!

The Abbey's rejection of his play *The Silver Tassie* in 1926 stunned O'Casey. He never really forgave, though Ireland was ready to forgive one of her finest playwrights and the most honest observer of the brave deeds he wrote about. O'Casey's supporters say he was misunderstood; others that he was understood all too well and found unacceptable. Not every Nationalist could easily reconcile the nobility of, for instance, Juno, with her pagan, inert politics.

After 1926 O'Casey lived mainly in England, where he died in 1964. In a tribute to him after his death the Abbey Theatre invoked the words of President Kennedy:

The artist has a lover's quarrel with the world. In pursuing his perceptions of reality he must often sail against the currents of his time. This is not a popular role.

# ENGLISH SETTLERS

Some of the occupying English had always supported Irish nationalism. These English settlers were called the Protestant Ascendancy, because the Anglo-Irish tended to dominate politically and culturally the native Irish. The Southern Ascendancy was a very small and widely dispersed minority. Many were landowners, or from that stock, before they arrived in Ireland while most Northern Protestants prospered after settling in Ulster. In the South the Anglo-Irish community co-existed in uneasy fellowship with the Irish, whose ways and manners a few tried to assimilate, sometimes successfully. Nevertheless the Anglo-Irish were always the English foreigners to the Irish, and more Irish than the Irish to their English connections.

The Easter Uprising generation of Anglo-Irish produced a number of sympathizers for Irish independence, such as Sir Roger Casement, Erskine Childers and Constance,

Countess Markievicz. Most were by nature Home-Rulers who were horrified by the lawlessness in Ulster. The Ulster Protestants were quite different from the rest of Ireland. They arrived in the seventeenth century, concentrated themselves in North-East Ulster and drove the Irish into the desolate regions to the West. They remained passionately loyal to England. Ulster did not want to be part of an independent Catholic Ireland, which Ulster thought it would probably have to subsidise, being much wealthier.

During the First Home Rule debate in 1886 Randolph Churchill warned: "Home Rule means Rome Rule. Ulster will fight and Ulster will be right." Churchill's warning echoed down the years. In the next generation Ulster discovered her own eloquent leader – Edward Carson – and he was succeeded by the intractable Edward Craig.

---

## Sir Roger Casement (1864-1916) and Erskine Childers (1874-1921)

---

Roger Casement and Erskine Childers were both passionate Irish Republicans and both were involved in raising money in England for their cause.

Roger Casement was born in Dublin, the son of an army officer. His parents died when he was young and he was brought up in Protestant Antrim. From an early age he showed deep concern for oppressed people and a bitterness towards authority which allowed such conditions to prevail. Once,

when travelling through the desolate regions of Donegal, he came across a young widow and child living in a squalid cabin. He gave money to the parish priest to buy her a cow so that "she always would have milk for her child".

He joined the Foreign Office and was knighted for his services in 1911, though the one service important to Casement was his exposure of the exploitation of native workers by European employers in the Congo and later in Peru. His fearless denunciation of colonial outrages won him international renown but notoriety in England. In 1903, when on leave, he met the Nationalists Bulmer Hobson and the well-known Belfast solicitor F.J. Bigger, and thereafter Irish independence became a burning issue with him. Casement was also attracted to Griffith's Sinn Féin. In 1913 he resigned from the Foreign Office on grounds of ill-health. He also wanted freedom from officialdom to press on with his work for Ireland. He was on the Committee of the Volunteers but never joined the I.R.B., and at this point, he persuaded Alice Stopford Green to form a London Committee to raise money to buy arms for the Volunteers. Mrs Stopford Green was a daughter of the Protestant Archdeacon of Meath. She was intensely nationalistic and a woman whose beauty, wit and intelligence fascinated a wide circle of friends, from the Conservative Arthur Balfour to the Socialist Beatrice Webb.

Practically everyone who met Casement was enchanted by his gentle manner and noble bearing. Typical of his impact on people is A.D. Morel's description of him. Morel was a politician who defeated W.S. Churchill in the 1922 General Election. He wrote:

. . . a long, lean, swarthy Van Dyke type, graven with power and with all of great gentleness. From the moment our hands gripped and our eyes met, mutual trust and confidence were bred. . . . Here was a man indeed.

The novelist, Joseph Conrad, met Casement in the Congo and was also impressed. There was, however, a darker side to his character – an unsteadiness of purpose, some instability in his nature and a delusion that he was Ireland's Messianic liberator. In 1914 Casement was in America and met the Irish-American leadership which was to finance his fund-raising mission to Germany later that year. He wrote:

They see me as a sort of aged Parnell. I can see from the way they greet me that they are setting their hearts on a Protestant leader, and think, poor brave souls, I may be the man.

Interestingly, John Devoy, the Irish-American leader, had serious doubts about Casement's fitness to lead the Uprising and

**45** Casement resented a government which had its subjects living in deprivation.

become Ireland's special envoy when he went to Germany.

A curious thing happened when Casement set out on his ill-fated journey to Germany. He insisted that a Norwegian seaman, called Adler Christensen, whom he had met casually in New York, should accompany him as his servant. Lurid rumours soon spread about the nature of their relationship. On the journey Casement suddenly had the conviction that the British Consul in Norway had offered Adler a £5000 bribe to kidnap or kill him. Whatever the truth of this mysterious business, Casement became obsessed to the point of paranoia with this imagined or otherwise threat. The experience unnerved him and, being anyway a somewhat neurotic man who did not enjoy the best of health, his self-styled ambassadorial role was almost a total failure.

He had come to an agreement, or Treaty as Casement self-deceptively called it, with the Germans, whereby Germany promised arms, the recruitment of an Irish brigade from Irish prisoners-of-war to provide the strike-force for the Uprising, and recognition of the Irish Republic if the Uprising was a success. But only 52 out of 2000 Irish prisoners took up his offer. He failed to get firm German encouragement except to supply arms. In 1916 Casement set out for Ireland to stop the Uprising. On the voyage the submarine captain, Raimund Weisback, observed Casement's, "increasing gloom respecting the Rising and a forboding of his own death". In the meantime, the British navy had captured the German ship carrying 20,000 rifles and ammunition to the rebels, and within hours of landing in Ireland Casement was arrested and taken to the Tower of London to wait trial for treason for collaboration with England's enemy. Casement's defence was that he was "taking his stand on Ireland's right to be free of Britain's law" and, on Bernard Shaw's suggestion, that as an Irishman he could not be accused of treason against England. Casement's speech from the dock inspired the future Indian leader, Pandit Nehru.

46 Casement urges Irish prisoners-of-war in Germany to join the forthcoming Uprising. Only 52 agreed.

An Empire that can only be held together by one section of its governing population perpetually holding down a smaller section must have some canker at its heart, some ruin at its root.

The jury reached a verdict of guilty, and Casement was condemned to death.

During the trial Casement's diaries, which revealed him as homosexual, were shown by the prosecuting counsel, F.E. Smith to the defence counsel, Sergeant Sullivan, in the hope that Sullivan would use this not altogether convincing evidence to make a plea of "guilty but insane". Sullivan knew "the government did not want to hang Casement in view of America's feeling towards Ireland. . . . The diaries might save Casement's life but a perverted diary would not in itself prove insanity." A medical board reported that Casement was "abnormal but not certifiably insane". The Foreign Office then circulated the diaries to Irish and Catholic newspaper editors in America hoping that Casement would be so discredited that moves of the

**47** Casement pleading "not guilty" to the charge of treason at the Old Bailey.

Very closely involved with the work of the London Committee formed by Alice Stopford Green to raise money for arms for the Volunteers was Erskine Childers. Childers was well connected: his mother was a Barton of Glendalough, County Wicklow, whose lovely ancestral house Childers always considered his home. An uncle had been Chancellor of the Exchequer in one of Gladstone's cabinets. From 1908 Childers was a hardened Home-Ruler. Churchill called him, "a mischief-making, murderous renegade," which shows the impossible position of the Anglo-Irish who tried to help Ireland without betraying England.

**48** Erskine Childers with his sons at Worthing, 1919. More republican than many Irish he was executed by the Irish Free State during the Civil War. His last words addressed to the firing squad were, "Take a step forward, gentlemen, you will find your job that much easier."

Irish-Americans to force a reprieve would be stifled. Theodore Roosevelt, (President, 1901-9), probably represented the wider American opinion when he wrote about the general Irish situation;

It was a prime necessity that the Uprising should be stamped out at once . . . but Carson himself and the Ulstermen had been so uncomfortably near to doing the same thing, and yet had been pardoned, that I think it would have been the better part of wisdom not to exact the death penalty in the case of those rebels. I don't include Casement whose case was wholly different.

The priest who gave Casement his last communion wrote: "He marched to the scaffold with the dignity of a prince and towered over all of us."

Childers was educated at Haileybury College and went to Trinity College, Cambridge. He possessed many talents and led a varied, active life. He fought for Britain in the Boer War and was an acknowledged authority on military matters about which he wrote copiously. For several years Childers had been a Clerk in the House of Commons. He is famous, too, as the author of the classic thriller, *The Riddle in the Sands* (published in 1903 and filmed in 1979), based on his sailing experiences along the

German North Sea coastline and which, uncannily, predicted England at war with Germany. His brilliance as a yachtsman was responsible for the gun-running success which armed the Irish Volunteers in July 1914.

On the outbreak of the Great War, while Casement was deeply immersed in his preparations for the Uprising, Childers joined the British navy, hoping that the Allies would support Irish independence. At the end of the war he returned to Irish affairs. In the 1919 Sinn Féin government he was elected T.D. for County Wicklow and became Minister for Propaganda in 1921.

Childers was secretary to the Irish delegation at the peace talks and was absolutely opposed to the signing of the Treaty. He became estranged from Griffith who unfairly accused "that Englishman" of intruding in Irish affairs. During the debate in the Dáil, Childers, "intellectually the most formidable opponent of the Treaty", exposed the flaws in the Treaty, one of which yielded control of four sea-ports to England.

During the Civil War, in which Childers joined the I.R.A. and took up the propaganda work for the anti-Treaty side, he was arrested. In Childers' possession was a revolver which Collins had given him as a token of comradeship in happier days. Possessing arms was a capital offence. The night before he was shot he begged his son to forgive "them", and wrote:

I die loving England, and praying she may change completely and finally towards Ireland.

He was granted an hour's reprieve to see the sun rise for the last time. His last act was to shake the hand of each member of the firing squad. Sadly, none of Childers' former Irish friends and close colleagues moved a hand to reprieve this Anglo-Irishman who gave no less for Ireland than did the greatest Irish patriots of those times. Perhaps Childers' mistake was to commit himself, an Anglo-Irish, more fiercely to the Republic than did some Gaelic-Irish. However, belated justice occurred in 1973 when Childers' son, also called Erskine, became President of the Republic of Ireland.

**49** Glendalough, Co. Wicklow, the ancestral home of Childers on his mother's side.

**50** The landing of arms for the Irish Volunteers in Dublin, 1914, from the yacht, *Asgard*, which had been one of the Childers' wedding presents. The aristocratic crew included Mary Rice Spring (right), daughter of Lord Monteagle and cousin to the British Ambassador in Washington. Childers' wife (left) was descended from John Adams, the second president of the U.S.A.

# Constance, Countess Markievicz (1868-1927)

Constance was born in London, the daughter of Sir Henry Gore-Booth. The family owned extensive estates in Ireland. Constance's early years followed the conventional pattern of the Anglo-Irish aristocracy which gave no hint of the radical direction her life later took. She was educated at home by a governess. In 1887 she was presented at Court and hailed "the new Irish beauty". She returned to Ireland where her charismatic presence, her fearlessness in the hunt and an eccentric manner were the talk, and envy, of house-parties. She was the best horsewoman in the West and was quite undaunted by eight-barred fences. She was also a fine shot and fascinated by the military arts – parades, uniforms and rituals. From 1898 to 1900 she studied art at the Slade School in London and in Paris. There, she met a Catholic Polish landowner called Casimir Markievicz who was six years younger than her. He, too, was a painter. Constance and Casimir were married in 1900. After travelling in France and the Ukraine (Casimir's homeland) they settled in Dublin in 1903.

The turning point in Constance's life happened by chance in 1906. She had rented a cottage and found a copy of the Gaelic League magazine which her predecessor had left behind. Constance immediately became conscious of Ireland's struggle for freedom and to the end of her life she dedicated herself, and sacrificed much personal happiness, to Ireland's cause. Constance joined Sinn Féin in 1905, though she and Griffith never liked each other: he was disconcerted by her domineering personality and aristocratic bearing. She was elected to the Sinn Féin Council and directed her energy to the sister movement, "Daughters of Ireland". This movement, formed by Maud Gonne, fought for women's rights, especially the vote. Constance also created her own movement called "Fianna". Similar to the Boy Scouts Fianna became an extreme nationalist youth organization. Constance trained the boys for a

51 Constance, Countess Markievicz at home in Dublin. She is wearing her Court "presentation" dress.

war of liberation. Each recruit declared, "I promise to work for the independence of Ireland, never to join England's armed forces, and to obey my superior officers". The boys were instructed in Irish history and the Irish language. Equal importance was given to physical and military training. Several Fianna

**52** The Countess seated with her Fianna boys, two of whom were shot after the Uprising.

boys became officers in the I.R.B. Two were among the 15 leaders executed after the Uprising.

Constance was always to be found where there was trouble. The 1913 Larkinite lockout strikes brought her in touch with Dublin's poverty and with Jim Larkin. After listening to him Constance wrote:

I realized that I was in the presence of something that I had never come across before, some great primeval force rather than a man. . . . It seemed as if his personality caught up, assimilated, and threw back to the vast crowd that surrounded him every emotion that swayed them, every pain and joy that they had ever felt made articulate and sanctified . . . this force of his magically changed the whole life of the workers in Dublin and the whole outlook of trade unionism in Ireland.

She sheltered Larkin in her home when he was a fugitive at the time he spoke disguised as a priest from the balcony of the Imperial Hotel. Later, she offered her home as refuge to Connolly. From that first meeting with Larkin Constance did all she could to help the poor. She identified with the workers' cause by joining the Citizen Army, in which she soon commanded a detachment. In addition, she organized soup kitchens during the strikes. As recently as the 1970s the Dublin poor remembered her with awe and affection. Ulick O'Connor once met in a pub an old crippled lady who, in spite of her infirmity, shuffled a jig on the floor. She turned to O'Connor and said: "I was taught by the Countess sixty years back." O'Connor records, "For a second a presence lit the room."

By 1916 Constance was a zealous activist in the Irish Volunteers. Her determination to contribute to all the Irish revolutionary movements seemed simplistic to some people. Sean O'Casey, who disliked her for similar reasons as Griffith, complained that no one in all sincerity could belong both to the Citizen Army and the Irish Volunteers, because their aims were so different. The Countess was in her element during the Uprising. She arrived to take up her position as second-in-command at Stephens Green in her open car, accompanied by two Fianna boys. She was the first to open fire on the English and the last to lay down her arms. She took great pride in keeping a record of "the number of Tommies whom she brought down". Constance defiantly refused to accept the order to surrender until she found herself virtually abandoned. She contemptuously turned aside

**53** Catholic Church support for Sinn Féin, when Father Dudley blessed the colours and flag on St Patrick's Day, March 1922.

**54** The Countess at her post during the Uprising.

an offer of a lift in a car telling the English officer she would march off to captivity at the head of her men. Much to Constance's fury she was spared execution because of her gender.

Constance was freed in the general amnesty of 1917. When she was elected T.D. for one of Dublin's constituencies in 1918 she became the first woman to be elected to the British Parliament. However, in keeping with Sinn Féin policy, she never sat in Westminster. In the "rebel" Sinn Féin government she was Minister of Labour. On the run from the security forces when England tried to suppress the Sinn Féin government she was imprisoned twice. She opposed the Anglo-Irish Treaty and toured America in 1922 to muster support for the Republic's cause. At this time Constance revitalized the Daughters of Ireland movement. The organization was fiercely republican and its aims were debated in the Dáil. It received the strong backing of

Erskine Childers, but so few male T.D.s contributed that wits called the organization "the women and Childers party".

Constance's republican ideals never weakened, in spite of her fourth term in prison (1923) under Cosgrave's pro-Treaty government, during which she went on hunger-strike. She joined de Valera's Fianna Party and was re-elected to the Dail in 1927. By then her health, which had been frail for some years, began to give way and the accumulated physical stress and social sacrifices took their toll. She died in July that year. Casimir, who had not lived in Dublin since 1907, hastened to her bedside.

By any measurement Constance was a remarkable woman. Yet, in the end, she was a victim of her circumstances – an Anglo-Irish who had thrown off her roots but was never at home among the Gaelic-Irish except the very poor.

She was not easy to work with – voluble, seemingly arrogant (though perhaps this masked the loneliness of a *déclassée*), and as the years went on, becoming more and more bitter and intense. (Leyland Lyons, *Ireland Since the Famine*)

# Edward Carson (1854-1935) and James Craig (1871-1940)

Outside Stormont Parliament in Belfast stands a statue of Edward Carson. This might seem odd because Carson was neither an Ulsterman nor had he succeeded in his life's ambition of maintaining the union of all Ireland with the United Kingdom. Carson used the Protestant stronghold of Ulster as a base to maintain the Irish parliamentary union with Britain – "the guiding star of my political life", he said. To this end Carson, a lawyer who was to rise to the top of his profession and hold ministerial rank, was prepared to defy the law of the land. He led Ulster to the very brink of civil war and came close to destroying the stability of Britain which it was his duty to preserve.

Edward Carson was born in Dublin. He was one of the finest lawyers of his generation in an age of great barristers. His grasp of a brief was masterly; in court his concise and dramatic

**55** Edward Carson inspired Ulster's resistance to Irish Home Rule.

**56** Carson signs Ulster's pledge to resist Home Rule.

advocacy ruined Oscar Wilde and acquitted the "Winslow" Boy. In the 1880s he won the admiration of Arthur Balfour (future Conservative prime minister) by his fearless prosecution of Irish people during the Land War (page 63). Balfour, then Chief Secretary, said, "Everybody right up to the top was trembling. . . . Carson had nerve." In 1900 he was Solicitor-General for England. His terse, incisive oratory and a rather forbidding yet charismatic presence – he was tall, gaunt, grim-faced and saturnine – captivated the dour Ulster mass-audiences.

In 1911 Carson gave his first speech as leader of the Ulster Unionists, which awed his Protestant audience and shocked the Government. Carson spoke before 50,000 Ulster people who had travelled from Orange Lodges and Unionist Clubs all over Ulster to hear the man whom they regarded as their protector against Irish Home Rule.

We are convinced that Home Rule would be disastrous to the material well-being of Ulster and all Ireland, subversive of our civil and religious freedom and perilous to the unity of the Empire. We must use all means which may be necessary to defeat the present conspiracy to set up a Home Rule parliament in Ireland. . . . The very morning Home Rule is passed, we must be prepared ourselves to become responsible for the government of the Protestant province of Ulster.

Cries of "No Surrender" greeted Carson's challenging words. Many people, especially in Southern Ireland, believed that Carson's seditious declaration was bluff. Redmond himself misunderstood Ulster's feelings, describing them as "a gigantic game of bluff and blackmail". Not so Bernard Shaw, who said,

Political opinion in Ulster is not a matter of talk and bluff, as it is in England. There is a strength in the Ulsterman's rancour which should be taken seriously.

As the Home Rule Bill made its slow, stormy way through the Commons, during which insults and books were hurled across the floor, Carson said on 11 February 1914,

. . . if [Ulster people] are not morally justified when they are being driven out of one government with which they are satisfied and put under another which they loathe, I do not see how resistance ever can be justified in history at all.

Lloyd George retorted that as Ireland would still have M.P.s in Westminster to debate the critical areas of government he saw no reason why Ulster should feel "driven out".

But Ulster feared that Home Rule today would lead to greater Irish independence tomorrow. In March 1914 the Government conceded the uniqueness of Ulster's position by offering a six years' opting out of Home Rule. Carson refused to accept "a sentence of death with a stay of execution for six years". In a combative speech at Bradford, Churchill threatened to put Ulster's loyalty "to the proof" by sending troops to disarm the Ulster Volunteers. Carson replied in withering fashion in the House of Commons and then left for Belfast. Many thought he had gone to raise a rebel government: more likely he left to evade arrest. But the Government admitted, "that any move against Ulster would be disastrous", especially in the light of the

**57** Carson (centre) at an Ulster anti-Home Rule demonstration. F.E. Smith, who prosecuted Casement, is on Carson's left.

58   James Craig was Ulster's first Prime Minister.

Conservative opposition and the suspect loyalty of the army to the elected government.

The Easter Uprising marked the time when Carson's policy fell apart. Carson had always assumed that Home Rule could not exist without Ulster. If Carson won Ulster's fight for exclusion from Home Rule, then Home Rule itself would abort. When it was evident that Home Rule for Southern Ireland would come in spite of Ulster, Carson's argument became ever closer identified with the narrow and sectarian obsessions of the North. No wonder Carson is often thought of as a fighter for Ulster separateness rather than for the preservation of Irish union with England. In this sense Carson became a prisoner of Ulster politics and, in the end, Ulster's victim.

In 1921 Carson was in poor health and resigned the leadership of the Ulster Unionists. Ulster had achieved the most she could expect and Carson's larger hopes for Ireland were beyond recall. He was never an easy colleague: his abrasive manner lost him friends and disconcerted his colleagues. The historian A.J.P. Taylor described Carson as "dangerous in opposition, ineffective in office".

J.C. Beckett in *Leaders and Men of the Easter Uprising* sums up the conflict within Carson and the final failure of his mission:

Although so much of Carson's political life was spent in opposing what most Irishmen wanted . . . Carson was a patriot without being a nationalist . . . he denied completely the existence of a distinct Irish nationality in any political sense.

James Craig was Northern Ireland's first Prime Minister. He represented all the characteristics of the Ulster Unionist in their extreme form. His words "What we have now, we hold against all combinations" summed up the spirit and the policy of Ulster which survives to this day.

Craig was the son of a prosperous whiskey distiller. He was a large, heavy man with a military bearing and blunt manner. Aggressively protective of Ulster's traditions, Craig became M.P. for Co-Down in 1906. When Home Rule threatened 300 years of Ulster Unionism Craig belligerently took up Ulster's cause. He invited Carson to lead Ulster's resistance, and organized the massive demonstration when Carson first alerted the British Government to the strength of Ulster feeling.

Once the Government accepted, for the time being, Ulster's special case all Craig had to do was sit tight – and at that he had no peer. Not even the beguiling persuasiveness of Lloyd George could weaken Craig's resolve. Craig condescended once to attend the Anglo-Irish talks. For two hours Lloyd George implored Craig to accept the independence of the Northern Ireland Parliament under Dublin's control. But Craig would not budge.

Craig never forgot how precarious Ulster's position was, and how vulnerable the Province was to shifting moods and attitudes of the British Government. In principle the British Government hoped for an Irish reunification one day. Naturally, Craig was obsessively suspicious of ideas like the Boundary Clause (page 12) which could tamper with Northern Ireland's status quo. "I will never give in to any rearrangement," Craig stated.

Protestant fear of the Catholic presence

**59** Sectarian strife in Belfast as Catholics protest against the partition of Ireland, 1920. In Southern Ireland the partition issue was very low-key. During the Treaty debate only nine papers out of 328 mentioned partition. The T.D.s hoped the Boundary Clause would eventually re-unite Ireland. De Valera knew, also, that the South was too shattered by recent fighting to coerce Ulster.

(around two-fifths of Ulster's population), founded on historic and recent events, was reflected in discrimination against Catholics in jobs and housing. And the manipulation of local elections maintained the Protestant-Ascendancy in local government. Resentment at Protestant "Apartheid" led to mounting tension and sectarian street battles. The struggle for civil rights and the benefits (which the Republic never matched) from the post-Second World War welfare state tended to become rather more important to Ulster's Catholics than re-unification with the South.

Craig was Prime Minister for 20 years and died in office in 1940. Time and time again he set on record Ulster's simple, unswerving commitment, "that come what may our position within the United Kingdom and the

**60** The consequence of political failure: refugees from Belfast arrive in Dublin.

Empire must remain unchanged". None of Craig's successors, except Terence O'Neill, have deviated from that narrow, inflexible vision of Protestant Ulster. Within that limitation Craig was an effective operator. But the consequences of the Protestant vision have led to the siege mentality of the Protestants, the conditioning of the Loyalist ethos and the mistrust and hostility of the Catholics. In the wings lurk the Provisional I.R.A., still working towards Patrick Pearse's dream, and when accused of violence by the British they reply that it is the presence and tyranny of the British in Northern Ireland which is the first act of violence.

# GLOSSARY

**The Curragh Incident** (misleadingly sometimes called "Mutiny") In March 1914 115 officers at the British garrison at the Curragh outside Dublin resigned when informed that military intervention might be necessary to enforce Home Rule in Ulster. They withdrew their resignation only after a written assurance from the Secretary of State for War that the Irish Command would not be so used. The full consequences of this situation were averted by the outbreak of the Great War, but the uncertainty of the army's loyalty, and the political interests of famous and revered soldiers, gravely limited the options and pressure Prime Minister Asquith could confidently use to bring Ulster into line with the decisions of Parliament, and he was forced to make special arrangements for Ulster.

**Dail Eireann** The Irish Parliament.

**Eire** Irish name for Ireland.

**Fenian** Member of the American branch of the I.R.B. (see below), which soon embraced the I.R.B. membership in Ireland. Name comes from a band of ancient Gaelic warriors.

**Gun-running** Illegal shipment of arms.

**"Hung" Parliament** Situation when no one political party commands an outright majority at an election. To stay in government the majority party needs the support of one or more of the other parties.

**Irish Conscription Act (1918)** This contentious Act meant that Irish males previously exempt, would have to join the British army and fight against Germany. The Act was never implemented because the Armistice in November stopped the fighting.

**Irish Home Rule** Limited self-government presided over by a Dublin Parliament within the British Empire. Crucial departments like Defence and Foreign policy would be decided in London. Ireland would be left with just Home Affairs issues.

**Irish Labour Party (I.L.P.)** Founded in 1914 by James Connolly, though Jim Larkin must share the credit for inspiring the political consciousness of the Irish workers in earlier years. The Party's aim was, wrote Connolly, "to transfer the political power of the state into the hands of those who will use it to further and extend the principle of common or public ownership". The means to political power was through the ballot box.

**Irish Nationalists** The historic political party which Parnell welded into a single-minded, coherent force in the 1890s. Since Parnell the Party represented moderate Irish opinion; devolution rather than separation from English rule, and constitutional means to achieve political ends such as Home Rule. After 1916 the Irish Nationalists were discredited and, in the 1918 General Election, destroyed.

**Irish Republican Army (I.R.A.)** Formed in 1917 from the Irish Volunteers (see below). The I.R.A. became the military wing of the political Sinn Féin once de Valera was elected president of both the civil and military branches.

**Irish Republican Brotherhood (I.R.B.)** Founded in 1858 as the most extreme republican movement. Aimed to liberate Ireland from English rule by armed force. The I.R.B. had very strong roots and backing in America. Many Irish-Americans had fled the horrors of the famine years in the 1840s. They nurtured intense hatred for England and were ever alert to events in Ireland. They provided funds, arms and soldiers when conditions for revolt seemed promising, and hope when rebellion failed – as it usually did. To this day, the Irish-American lobby is very strong. The I.R.B. planned and led the Easter Uprising.

**Irish Volunteers** The armed force raised in Southern Ireland (1913) by Eoin MacNeill to fight for Irish Home Rule.

**Land Wars** (1879-82) Revolt of Irish tenant farmers under Fenian Michael Davitt against English landlords. Davitt called his organization the Land League (1880). The Land War flared up in earnest when the police and soldiers were sent to enforce landlords' rights. Evictions and retaliations followed on a massive scale. Secret terror gangs, called "Captain Moonlight", stalked the countryside maiming cattle, burning crops, intimidating, and soon assassinating, bailiffs and landlords. The Land War faded when Parnell agreed to try to stop the rural terror, provided that Gladstone (the Liberal Prime Minister) introduced measures in Parliament to relieve the distress of the most vulnerable tenants and provide them with better security of tenancy.

**Loyalist Ethos** The state of mind of Ulster Unionists brought about by their phobia of losing political control to Catholic Ireland with or without the collusion of a British government. The manifestations of this condition are an intense, perhaps infantile, loyalty to the British monarch (not necessarily to the government in office), an obsessional need for belonging to the U.K., and a dread of being "sold out" to the Catholic Irish.

**Orange Order** Named after the Protestant King William of Orange (William III of England) whose army saved Londonderry from the Catholics (1689). Originally a working-class movement, it came to attract all classes and became the centre of grass-root Ulster Protestant resistance to Catholic attempts to undermine the Protestant Ascendancy (see below).

**Partition** Dividing a country into two parts.

**Patriot** Defender of his/her country's rights or freedom.

**Protestant Ascendancy** Principle of preserving the political dominance of the minority Protestants in Catholic Ireland.

**Republic** A state without a monarch, in which supreme power is invested in elected representatives or an elected head of state.

**Sinn Féin** Means "Ourselves"; sometimes, but mistakenly, "Ourselves Alone". The political movement founded by Arthur Griffith (1905). Easily, but wrongly, confused with the much older movement, the I.R.B. (see above). Sinn Féin only became republican when it merged with the I.R.B. in 1917 under de Valera.

**Socialism** The belief that a nation's wealth and the means of creating it should be owned by the state for the benefit of the people.

**Status quo** Unchanged position; here referring to the Empire.

**Teachtei Dela (T.D.)** Elected member of the Irish Parliament.

**Ulster Volunteers** The para-military force raised to fight Home Rule and keep Protestant Ulster within the United Kingdom under the Westminster Parliament.

**Unionist** Any person or group which supported the preservation of Irish union with the U.K. The Unionists tended to be concentrated in Ulster where in six of the N.E. counties they outnumbered the indigenous Irish. In England the strongest Unionist support came from the Conservative and Unionist Party and, by sentiment, the military establishment.

# DATE LIST

**1905**    Arthur Griffith founds Sinn Féin.

**1910**

December    General Election returns a "hung" Parliament. Asquith's Liberal Party dependent on Irish Nationalists' support to stay in office.

**1911**

August    Parliament Act passed which limits the power of the House of Lords. The Lords can delay for only two years Bills from the House of Commons.

**1912**    John Redmond, leader of the Irish Nationalists, threatens to withdraw Irish support unless the Liberals introduce a Home Rule Bill.

April    Asquith introduces third Home Rule Bill. Certainty of Bill becoming law rallies the opposition.
Edward Carson warns huge rally in Belfast that Ulster will never accept Home Rule.

July    Andrew Bonar Law, leader of the Conservative Party, supports Ulster in a contentious speech at Blenheim Palace.

September    Half a million Ulster people pledge their opposition to Home Rule.

**1913**    Larkinite lock-out strikes in Dublin.

January    Ulster Volunteers, a para-military force, raised to resist Home Rule in Ulster.

November    Irish Volunteers formed in Dublin.

**1914**    Patrick Pearse and the I.R.B. plan Uprising. They intend to use the Irish Volunteers to spearhead the revolt.

March    The Curragh "Mutiny". Many officers prefer to resign than march north and possibly fight Ulster "loyalists". Resignations withdrawn when the War Office assures disaffected officers that the army would not be used to force Ulster to accept Home Rule. Asquith is not told about this arrangement. Minister of War resigns.

April    Gun-running arms the Ulster Volunteers.

July    Arms landed at Houth, near Dublin, for the Irish Volunteers. The gun-runners are surprised by The King's Own Scottish Borderers. Volunteers escape with most of the weapons. British soldiers so riled by the taunts of Irish civilians that they fire into crowd, killing three civilians and wounding nearly 40.

August    Britain at war with Germany. Redmond pledges Irish support for Britain's war effort.
Irish Volunteers split up. Most follow Redmond. By helping England in her hour of need Redmond hopes to keep British support for Home Rule. Small minority stay with Eoin MacNeill, including members of the militant I.R.B., who are well placed in the Volunteers' high command.

September    Home Rule suspended until after the War.

**1915**    Funeral of Jeremiah O'Donovan Rossa in Dublin. Pearse gives the oration.

**1916**

January    British Government rejects conscription for Ireland.
James Connolly, Irish labour leader, agrees to support the Uprising.

9 April    The *Aud* sails from Germany with arms for the Volunteers.

10 April    Augustine Birrell, Chief Secretary for Ireland, assures the Government "I do not believe Irish Volunteers mean insurrection."

19-22 April    *Aud* intercepted by British patrol boats. Captain scuttles *Aud*; all arms lost.
Roger Casement lands in Ireland

from a German submarine. He is arrested within hours.

In Dublin, MacNeill is shown the Castle Document, which states that the English are about to disarm the Volunteers.

MacNeill discovers the "Document" may have been forged by the I.R.B. to force MacNeill to mobilize the Volunteers.

The Uprising is due to start on 23 April, Easter Sunday. MacNeill hears about the arms loss, Casement's failure to recruit Irish prisoners-of-war and Casement's arrest.

MacNeill orders the Volunteers not to rebel. Pearse and the I.R.B. postpone the Uprising to Easter Monday.

| | |
|---|---|
| 24 April | Patrick Pease declares the Republic of Ireland from the steps of the G.P.O. in Dublin at noon. Of the seven signatures to the document four were writers. |
| 24-29 April | 1600 Irish Volunteers hold out against British soldiers. By the time Pearse surrenders the centre of Dublin is in smoking ruins. Irish deeply outraged at the Uprising. |
| 3-12 May | 15 revolutionary leaders executed on order of General Sir John Maxwell, the military governor in Ireland. |
| 17 May | Bishop of Limerick is the first public figure to denounce the executions. |
| 25 May | Asquith entrusts David Lloyd George with the Irish "problem". Lloyd George's initiative obstructed by Unionists. Redmond and the Irish Nationalists discredited by Lloyd George's failure to achieve Home Rule for all Ireland. Support grows for Sinn Féin. |
| July | The British suffer homicidal losses during the Battle of the Somme. |
| December | Lloyd George succeeds Asquith as Prime Minister. First group of revolutionaries released, including Collins. |

**1917**

| | |
|---|---|
| April | U.S.A. declares war on Germany. |
| June | Last of Easter 1916 insurgents released from prison, including de Valera. |
| July | De Valera wins Clare by-election for Sinn Féin. |
| September | Funeral of Thomas Ashe, a re-arrested Volunteer who died in prison. |
| October | Sinn Féin becomes official political heir to Uprising's revolutionaries. Irish Volunteers become the State army, the Irish Republican Army (I.R.A.). De Valera becomes head of both organizations. |

**1918**

| | |
|---|---|
| April | Irish Conscription Bill passed. Irish Nationalists withdrawn in protest from House of Commons. Uproar in Ireland. |
| May | Field Marshal Sir John French sent to pacify Ireland. Many Sinn Féin leaders arrested. |
| November | Germany surrenders. End of Great War. |
| December | General Election. Sinn Féin majority party in Ireland. |

**1919**

| | |
|---|---|
| January | Sinn Féin sets up own government in Dublin. British institutions ignored. Shooting of two Royal Irish Police-men by the I.R.A. precipitates the Anglo-Irish War. Collins organizes his "Assassination squad". |
| March | "Black and Tans", drawn from British ex-servicemen, arrive in Ireland. |
| November | "Bloody Sunday". |
| December | Burning of Cork by "Tans". |

**1921**

| | |
|---|---|
| July | King opens Northern Ireland Parliament in Belfast. James Craig becomes first Prime Minister of the province. Truce is agreed in the South. |
| December | Anglo-Irish Treaty signed by Collins and Griffith. |

**1922**

| | |
|---|---|
| January | The Dáil accepts Treaty terms by a majority of seven. De Valera |

| | | | |
|---|---|---|---|
| August | denounces Treaty. I.R.A. is split. Civil War follows. Death of Griffith and Collins. William Cosgrave heads the Irish Free State Government. | November 1923 | Childers executed. 77 executions by Free State from November 1922 to May 1923. End of Civil War. De Valera in temporary political isolation. |

# BIOGRAPHICAL NOTES

**Asquith,** Henry (1852-1928). Liberal Prime Minister from 1908 to 1916. Introduced the Third Irish Home Rule Bill (1912). His heart wasn't really with Irish affairs but in the "hung" Parliament (1910) Asquith needed the support of the Irish Nationalists for the Liberals to stay in office.

**Bonar Law,** Andrew (1858-1923). Leader of the Conservatives; later Prime Minister. Unlike most politicians of the day, Bonar Law knew Ulster well and sympathized with the Province's anxieties on Home Rule. He threw the weight of the Conservative Party behind Ulster's resistance to Home Rule.

**Breen,** Dan (1858-1923). A republican activist all his life whose shooting of two policemen in January 1919 sparked off the Anglo-Irish War. A great admirer of Collins, Breen turned against him and joined the dissident Irish who could not accept the terms of the Anglo-Irish Peace Treaty.

**Clarke,** Tom (1857-1916). An I.R.B. activist, convicted and imprisoned for bombings in England. Much of the planning for the Uprising and the liaison with America took place in Clarke's tobacconist shop. Signed the Declaration of the Irish Republic. Executed.

**Cosgrave,** William (1880-1965). Prime Minister of the Irish Free State on death of Collins and Griffith (1922). His Government resolutely waged war against I.R.A. rebels until de Valera surrendered.

**Devoy,** John (1842-1928). Member of the I.R.B. since its inception and sustained the movement when its first leaders were in prison or exile.

Became bitterly resentful of the indecision of I.R.B. leadership, which he believed had wasted vital chances of overthrowing English rule. Moved to America and became a leading figure in the Irish-American community.

**Dillon,** John (1851-1927). Irish Nationalist M.P. who succeeded John Redmond as leader of the Irish Nationalist Party. He urged toleration and moderation on the British Government when the Uprising was suppressed.

**Gonne,** Maud (1866-1953). Anglo-Irish of extreme republican sympathies. Daughter of a British officer, she was a well-known "beauty" and actress, and acted in Yeats' plays. Yeats was devoted to Maud. She married Major John MacBride, who had fought for the Boers against England and was executed after the Uprising.

**Gregory,** Lady Augusta (1852-1932). Of Anglo-Irish land-owning stock, she was also very close to grass-root Gaelic-Irish opinion. One of the inspirations behind the revival of Irish literature and, with Yeats, established the Abbey Theatre. She encouraged promising and unknown Irish writers, notably Sean O'Casey, and supported Yeats during his early difficult years.

**Larkin,** James (1876-1947). The formidable fighter for Irish labour who inspired James Connolly's socialism. His excessive methods and fiery temperament failed to win solidarity from the relatively moderate English union leaders.

**MacDonagh,** Thomas (1879-1916). Poet, revolutionary, friend to Pearse, at whose school he taught, and to Plunkett, whom he taught

Gaelic. A playwright of much promise. He once surprised his students when, during a lecture, he placed a revolver on his desk saying, "Ireland can only win freedom by force." He was one of seven signatories to the Declaration of the Irish Republic. Executed.

**O'Higgins,** Kevin (1892-1927). Perhaps the most promising politician of the post-Easter Uprising generation. A very tough political operator who, as reciprocal atrocities mounted in the Civil War, endorsed the execution of Rory O'Connor, his best man. Shot down in Dublin's streets.

**O'Neill,** Captain Terence (1914- ). Prime Minister of Northern Ireland 1963-9, who worked for inter-community tolerance. Lost support of both Catholics and Protestants.

**Parnell,** Charles Stewart (1848-91). Protestant land-owner, educated in England. Despite unlikely background, elected leader of the Irish Nationalist Party and became the most dominant politician of his generation. Succeeded in unifying Irish groups traditionally in conflict. His 86 Nationalist M.P.s held balance of power in 1886 General Election and he won over 200 English M.P.s to Home Rule that year. Hailed by Irish as "uncrowned King of Ireland", but deposed and discredited by his party once his ten-year adulterous relationship with Mrs Katherine O'Shea was publicly exposed. Reputation restored, only after his death, by next generation (particularly Yeats and Pearse) who felt Ireland had betrayed one of the finest Irish patriots. Has become something of a myth in Irish history.

**Plunkett,** Joseph (1887-1916). Son of a Papal count and director of the National Museum. On health grounds he spent winters in North Africa and became fascinated by Moorish culture: he always wore jewellery, even in Volunteers' uniform. Precociously intelligent, with an aptitude for soldiering he, like his friends Pearse and MacDonagh, was also a talented poet. One of the seven signatories to the Declaration of the Irish Republic, he was executed after the Uprising.

**Redmond,** John (1856-1918). Became leader of the Irish Nationalist Party in 1900. Healed the wounds in the Party after the split which followed Parnell's deposition in 1890. Redmond's conciliatory approach to England was more and more out of place with the gathering forces of militant republicanism which swept Ireland after the 1916 Uprising.

**Wavell,** Field Marshal Archibald (1883-1950). Staff officer at the War Office. Very critical of the army's subversive attitude to Ulster's position. Became a Field Marshal in World War II and was famous as a soldier belonging to the scholar-warrior tradition.

**Wilson,** Field Marshal Sir Henry (1864-1922). Director of Military Operations. A "political" soldier with extreme Unionist loyalties who undermined the army's role during the Ulster crisis. Shot down outside his London home by the I.R.A.

# BOOKS FOR FURTHER READING

## General Books

*Paul Arthur, *Government and Politics in North Ireland*, Longman, 2nd edition 1984

Richard Bennett, *The Black and Tans*, 1961

Owen Dudley Edwards and Fergus Pyle (eds.), *1916, The Easter Uprising*, MacGibbons and Kee, 1968. (An interesting series of essays especially on little-known aspects such as Lenin's reflections on the Rising and John Dillon's speech in the House of Commons questioning Asquith's knowledge of the executions)

J.G. Farrell, *Troubles*, Penguin, 1975 (A very fine novel by a Booker Prize winner [1973]. The book provides a sympathetic and fascinating insight into an Anglo-Irish family whose hereditary home and lifestyle is dissolving around them during the Anglo-Irish War.)

Sir James Fergusson, *The Curragh Incident*, Faber, 1964. (An excellent and detailed insight into a little-known but important episode of the times. The author is the son of the commander of 5 Division, where the officer protest against possible operations in Ulster began.)

*The Irish Question*, Schools Council History 13-16 Project, Holmes McDougall, 1977

Thomas Jones, *Whitehall Diary*, Vol. 3: *Ireland 1918-1925*, O.U.P., 1971 (A very important contribution to Irish affairs of the times because Thomas Jones as Deputy-Secretary to the Cabinet sat in on all the secret Government meetings and negotiations at the Peace talks)

Robert Kee, *Ireland: A History*, Sphere, 1982

Robert Kee, *The Green Flag Vol. 3: Ourselves Alone*, Quartet Books, 1976

Lord Longford and Ann Mchardy, *Ulster*, Weidenfeld, 1981

F.S.L. Lyons, *Ireland since the Famine*, Collins/Fontana, 1973 (A scholarly and readable book with excellent accounts of the period)

F.X. Martin (ed.) *Leaders and Men of the Easter Rising*, Methuen, Dublin, 1916

Wick O'Connor, *A Terrible Beauty is Born*, Panther, 1981. (A very readable account of the Uprising and the participants.)

F. Packenham, *Peace by Ordeal*, Weidenfeld, 1972. (The making of the Anglo-Irish Treaty)

E.G. Power, *Then and There: The Easter Uprising and Irish Independence*, Longman, 1979

Robert Rhodes James, *The British Revolution Vol. 1: 1880-1914*, 1976; *Vol. 2: 1914-1939*, 1977, Hamish Hamilton (The sections on Ireland are clearly and fluently expressed. Vol. 1 covers the Third Home Rule Bill crisis 1912-14.)

A.J.P. Taylor, *English History 1914-1945*, Oxford University Press, 19xx

*Charles Townsend, *Political Violence in Ireland* O.U.P, 1983

Desmond Williams (ed.), *The Irish Struggle 1916-1926*, Routledge and Kegan Paul, 1966

Carlton Younger, *Ireland's Civil War*, Fontana, 1970 (Provides a readable account of the Easter Uprising and Anglo-Irish War)

* More suitable for students studying Ireland in some depth.

## Visionaries

Ruth Dudley Edwards, *Patrick Pearse: The Triumph of Failure*, Gollancz, 1977

Michael Tierney, *Eoin MacNeill: Scholar and Man of Action 1867-1945*, Oxford University Press, 1980

Carlton Younger, *Gill's Irish Lives: Arthur Griffith*, Gill and Macmillan, Dublin, 1981

## Politicians

T. Ryle Dwyer, *Gill's Irish Lives: Eamon de Valera*, Gill and Macmillan, Dublin, 1980

Ruth Dudley Edwards, *Gill's Irish Lives: James Connolly*, Gill and Macmillan, Dublin, 1981

C. Desmond Greaves, *The Life and Times of James Connolly*, Lawrence and Wishart, 1976

John Grigg, *Lloyd George Vol. 3, 1985* (Has two chapters which cover the struggle for third Home Rule Bill and Uprising. Vol. 4 [not yet published] should cover the Anglo-Irish War and Peace Treaty. A very readable account.)

Leon O'Broin, *Gill's Irish Lives: Michael Collins*, Gill and Macmillan, Dublin, 1980

A.J.P. Taylor (ed.), *Lloyd George: Twelve Essays*. (Includes an excellent chapter on Lloyd George's involvement with Ireland 1916-1921)

**Writers**

Gabriel Fallon, *Sean O'Casey: The Man I Knew*, Routledge and Kegan Paul, 1965

R.J. Finnevan, *Yeats: The Poems*, Macmillan, 1984

George S. Fraser, *Writers and Their Work: W.B. Yeats*, Longman, 1963

Hugh Hunt, *Gill's Irish Lives: Sean O'Casey*, Gill and Macmillan, Dublin, 1980

David Krause, *Sean O'Casey and his World*, Thames and Hudson, 1976

Augustine Martin, *Gill's Irish Lives: William Butler Yeats*, Gill and Macmillan, Dublin, 1983

Sean O'Casey, *Three Plays*, Pan, 1980

**English Settlers**

Andrew Boyle, *The Riddle of Erskine Childers*, Hutchinson, 1978

Patrick Buckland, *Gill's Irish Lives: James Craig*, Gill and Macmillan, Dublin, 1980

Brian Inglis, *Roger Casement*, Hodder and Stoughton, 1973

Anne Marreco, *The Rebel Countess: The Life and Times of Constance Markievicz*, Weidenfeld and Nicolson, 1967

A.T.Q. Stewart, *Gill's Irish Lives: Edward Carson*, Gill and Macmillan, Dublin, 1983

# INDEX